Music Revision for

Leaving Certificate

Andrew Purcell

Gill & Macmillan Ltd
Hume Avenue
Park West
Dublin 12
with associated companies throughout the world
www.gillmacmillan.ie

© Andrew Purcell 2006
© Artwork Halstan Music Setting and Printing and Peter Bull Art Studio
ISBN-13: 978 0 7171 3985 9
ISBN-10: 0 7171 3985 9
Print origination in Ireland by Carole Lynch

The paper used in this book is made from the wood pulp of managed forests. For every tree felled, at least one tree is planted, thereby renewing natural resources.

Contents

1 How the Exam is Marked

There are 400 marks (100%) available in total for the entire Leaving Certificate Music examination.

Core Practical

This accounts for 100 marks, or 25% of the total. It usually takes place around Easter.

Listening Paper I

Marks available: 100 marks, or 25% of the total. These are distributed as follows:

- Set Works:
  1 Question 1 (Long Question): 25 marks, or 6.25% of the complete exam
  2 Questions 2, 3 and 4: 30 marks, or 7.5% of the complete exam
- **Question 5 (Irish Music): 25 marks, or 6.25% of the complete exam**
- **Question 6 (Aural Skills): 20 marks, or 5% of the complete exam.**

Composition Paper II

Marks available: 100 marks, or 25% of the total, distributed as follows:

- Melody (Question 1, 2 or 3): 40 marks, or 10% of the complete exam
- Harmony (Question 4, 5 or 6): 60 marks, or 15% of the complete exam.

Elective: Practical, Listening or Composition

This accounts for 100 marks, or 25% of the total.

Higher Level: choose [i]one[ei] Elective from:

- **Practical (done with Core Practical, around Easter)**
- **Composition (portfolio work)**
- **Listening (written paper on the day of the exam).**

Ordinary Level candidates do not have to take an elective. Their highest mark in core listening, composition or practical will be doubled to make up the extra 25%.

2 Practice and Performance Tips

Remember that your performance can account for up to 50% of your Leaving Certificate exam, so you must give your performance the practice it deserves over the two years of preparing for the exam. The best performers are usually those who use their practice time most effectively.

Here are some tips for effective practice:

- choose a time when you are well rested and your enthusiasm is high; for example, in the morning before going to school
- a pleasant atmosphere, with no noise or interruptions, is most conducive to concentration
- try to find a comfortable, quiet place to practise
- good air circulation and good lighting are very important.

Self-evaluation is a must for improvement. Performing music is for the ear. You want to sound better. So, above all, remember to *listen to yourself*. Make your judgments and adjustments based on what you hear, so try to:

Record Yourself

Record your playing often. It should be an ear-opening experience. You should record yourself at different stages along the way. Then listen carefully and decide what you need to do to make your performance better.

Advantages: it improves your ability to listen. You can hear and judge your own playing instead of relying on somebody else to do it. By listening to your old recordings, you can hear the improvement you've made.

Remember: do it right from the very beginning. Always aim for perfection in notes, sound, and musical expression.

Try to Understand the Music

Look for the key, scales, chords, patterns, repeated sections, the form, phrases, accompaniment patterns, rhythmic patterns etc. Analysing the meaning of something helps you remember it longer.

Write Things Down

It helps you remember things better if you write them down. When you see what you've written a day, two days or a week later, it refreshes your memory and helps you retain the information permanently.

Create Your own Style by Interpretation

Circle all the dynamics and tempo markings. Write in your music how you want to play the piece.

Look at Practising as Problem Solving

Don't view practising as repeating your pieces a certain number of times. Look at practising as finding and solving problems.

Remember the 'five times easier' rule:

It is five times easier to learn it right the first time than to re-learn it after learning it wrong.

3 The Music Practical Exam

1   First impressions are important.
2   Look and *feel confident* from the moment you walk into the room/hall.
3   Choose to perform pieces that are not too difficult for your ability. Choosing something that you can perform fluently and performing it well will build your confidence throughout your performance.
4   Controlled nerves are good.
5   Don't forget to breathe – not just singers, all performers!
6   Be so prepared that you can play/sing/conduct with comfort and ease, so practise, practise and practise.
7   No matter how you feel you have performed, this element of the exam is not over until you exit the room or hall. Last impressions are important too.

> The most important tip is to be *over-prepared*. You should be able to perform the piece in your sleep! If you are over-prepared, you will be as confident as you can possibly be, but you should not perform your pieces as if you are totally bored with them! All your pieces must have a musical vibrancy and life about them.

Performance Requirements

If you are taking a higher level elective practical (six or eight pieces), be aware of the *time limit* involved. Each student gets a maximum time to perform all of his/her pieces and this is also true of the aural/sightreading tests.

Approximate Timings
Ordinary level: 10 minutes.

Higher level (elective): 15 minutes (25 minutes in total).

This is what is expected of you:

OL – Ordinary level. Two songs or pieces and one unprepared test.
H1 – Higher level, core (one performing activity). Three songs or pieces and one unprepared test.
H2 – Higher level, core (two performing activities). Two songs or pieces *in each* performing activity and one unprepared test.
HE1 – Higher level, elective (one performing activity). Six songs or pieces and one unprepared test.
HE2 – Higher level, elective (two performing activities). Four songs or pieces *in each* performing activity and one unprepared test.

- Harmony, where appropriate, must be an integral part of group singing.
- In any group performance (including traditional group), a maximum of *two* candidates per individual part is allowed.
- Solo and group performing are regarded as separate performing activities.
- Piano and electronic keyboard, acoustic guitar and six-string electric guitar, concert flute and traditional flute, flute and piccolo or any combination of recorders or any combination of percussion instruments may *not* be presented as two different activities, unless one is a solo and the other a group activity.
- Accompaniment or duet performance is treated as group performance.
- The same music may not be presented for two different activities.

Aural Tests

This accounts for 5% of the overall exam (20 marks of your practical exam).

You can choose:

1 sightreading (on instrument or voice)
2 aural memory rhythm (clapping back)
3 aural memory melody (singing back)
4 improvisation.

You can choose to do these aural test on a different instrument (medium) from the one you have played/sung for your music practical examinations.

Get your teacher to practise the aural memory tests with you, if you are not taking sight-reading or improvisation. These are worth 20 marks for all levels of exam candidate.

Past years' tests are available on the State Examinations Commission website: www.examinations.ie.

Sightreading

Look at the time signature, key signature and tempo indications first. Then quickly look over the music you are about to play. Ask yourself these questions:

- Are there any tempo changes, modulations, patterns, either rhythmic or melodic?
- What are the difficulties, if any?
- What are the dynamic indications?

Also remember:

- *Keep your place no matter what*, even if it means missing notes and/or rhythms.
- Go for an overall effect.

- Don't be tentative. Play convincingly; give the impression you know what you're doing.
- Stay calm!

4 Irish Traditional Music

Question 5, Paper I

This involves:

- identification of dance and vocal styles
- identification of instrumental timbres
- knowledge of Irish traditional musical characteristics
- knowledge of past and ongoing developments and styles in Irish traditional music.

Some common questions when listening to an Irish music extract:

- name the instruments as they enter, *or* name the melody instruments and the harmony/rhythm instruments in this extract
- name the type of dance being played
- what traditional characteristics can you hear in this extract?

History of Irish Traditional Music

Medieval to Early Seventeenth Century
Irish society consisted of the aristocracy, the commoners and the professional learned class, which included the fili or poets and the reacaire (harpist). European styles of Renaissance and early baroque music failed to influence the Irish tradition.

Seventeenth to Eighteenth Centuries: Two Traditions
Fiddlers, pipers and ballad singers thrived in this era and their cultural musical tradition was the mainstay of the Irish people. The musical traditions of the 'Big Houses' and the middle class inside the Pale were becoming more influenced by Italian classical music, including operas and oratorios. The Belfast harp festival of 1792 was organised to 'revive and perpetuate the Ancient Music and Poetry of Ireland'.

Nineteenth Century: Emigration and the Deterioration of Irish Music Culture
The famine and the mass emigration that followed it caused a led to the decline of musicians, dance masters and in the usage of the Irish language. Much traditional folklore was lost within the country, but traditional Irish music became part of the fabric of life from the USA to Australia. During this time many traditional tunes and songs were anglicised and became part of the culture of the middle and upper classes.

Twentieth-Century Revival of Irish Traditional Music
With national independence and with slow but steady economic development, a new breed of traditional musician was born; one who could revive old folklore and interpret it

for the world of the twentieth century. Ceili bands formed, radio and television programmes and recordings promoted the tradition like never before; and Sean O'Riada and Comhaltas Ceoltoiri Eireann (CCE) initiated structures that helped to develop a positive attitude towards Irish traditional music that has increased over the last few decades.

Characteristics of Irish Traditional Music (Past and Present)

1   In past eras, usually *no* harmony (apart from drones) – nowadays harmony (guitar, piano, vocal harmony etc.) can be an integral part of traditional styles.
2   Ornamentation (grace notes, slides, turns, rolls, replacing long notes with repeated notes and cuts) is usually used in traditional music.
3   Tempo, dynamics and other musical expressive effects are not usually used in traditional music.
4   Traditional music was usually a *solo* art form, but nowadays it is usually performed by groups or ensembles.
5   Most Irish traditional dance music is in a major key (tonality) but minor and modal (modes and gapped scales) are also found, especially in traditional singing.
6   Melodies (both sung and dance melodies, and usually in the treble clef) have a wide range.
7   The last note of a dance tune is often repeated at the end.
8   Irish traditional music is an *aural* tradition – passed on and taught by ear. Nowadays, many traditional songs and dances are notated down and so are accessible to musicians all over the world.
9   The texture of Irish traditional music was *monophonic*, but nowadays most session music and recordings are *homophonic* (melody with accompaniment); it is rarely, if ever, polyphonic.

Traditional Terminology

Bodhrán – simple frame drum (made with goat skin), which is beaten with a double-sided stick or the hand (fingers or knuckles).
CCE (Comhaltas Ceoltoiri Eireann) – a club set up in 1951 to promote Irish traditional music and dancing.
Ceili – a social occasion for traditional dancing.
Collector(s) – a person or institution (such as RTE, BBC) who notates (and nowadays records) the music and words of traditional music, songs and dances. This is a vital role in preserving a living aural tradition.
Fleadh Cheoil – the biggest annual festival of Irish traditional music with street sessions, classes in music, singing and dancing and concerts and competitions. Run by Comhaltas Ceoltoiri Eireann.

Hyberno-jazz – fusion of traditional Irish music with jazz characteristics.

Lilting – a singer sings a tune using nonsense words.

Sean nós – old style of traditional singing.

Session – a group or gathering of traditional musicians (and/or singers) to participate in music-making and fun.

Vamping – a type of piano accompaniment used in traditional music; usually the player plays simple chordal accompaniment patterns.

Characteristics of Sean Nós Singing

This 'old style' of traditional singing is unique to Ireland. It is a highly skilled solo art form that dates back many centuries. Themes and stories of the songs are usually about human life: birth, love, suffering, emigration and death.

Characteristics are:

1 solo singing
2 usually no dynamics, expression or vibrato
3 the most important things are the words and the story being told – the rhythm of the song is dictated by speech/syllable patterns
4 there is often an emphasis on the consonants l, m, n and r to facilitate the free rhythmic pulse and to create a drone effect
5 there are both Irish and English language songs in existence, even some with a mixture of both languages
6 ornamentation is generally used
7 there is not much repetition in songs
8 the glottal stop/dramatic pause is used
9 modal scales are often used
10 a nasal tone quality (nasalisation) is sometimes used
11 there is no strict tempo employed in the songs – free non-metronomic rhythm and rubato tempo
12 melismatic singing – use of many notes to one syllable
13 slow airs, played in imitation of *sean nós* songs, are played with very loose time signatures.

Each singer may have their own unique style but there are three general styles nationally:

Regional Styles of Sean Nós Singing

Ulster style:

■ smaller range of song
■ little ornamentation

Connaught style:

- lots of ornamentation
- use of nasal tone quality

Munster style:

- more like classical singing
- wider range in songs
- some ornamentation used

The English Language Song Tradition

The Irish song tradition is diverse and rich and enjoys a prominent place among the interrelated song traditions of Scotland, England and North America. Many traditional Irish songs are not sean nós-style songs. There have been many hundreds of folk songs and ballads passed down from generation to generation over the past two centuries. Dance tunes are sometimes also 'lilted', that is, sung with nonsense syllables. Many composed folk songs and ballads of the 1960s and 1970s have also become incorporated into this tradition. A huge variety of modern traditional styles can be said to come under the heading of 'traditional songs', from the rebel songs of the Dubliners to the popular ballads of Mary Black to Liam Ó Maonlaí's imaginative vocal fusion.

Regional Styles

Musical style in performance is a matter of personal interpretation. Different styles are distinguishable by the musical elements the musicians use – tempo, dynamics, amount of ornamentation used, and also the playing or singing techniques, phrasing and articulation.

In an aural tradition, players and singers have always developed the tunes that they learned by ear. This has led to many melodically similar tunes throughout the country with different titles or texts.

Before the advent of modern media, especially radio, Irish music was a local and rural tradition (apart from the tradition that emigrated to the cities of England and America).

There was no national 'Irish' style of playing or singing throughout the country. There were only distinct regional styles. These different styles still exist, for example the fiddle-playing techniques of Donegal, Galway and Sligo and the sean nós singing of the provinces of Munster, Connaught and Ulster.

Fusion

Fusion is a mixture of different musical styles and traditions. Irish traditional music has been fused with many different styles of music: jazz, pop, classical and rock. Other genres of fusion include a mixture of African drumming and traditional Irish dance music, or Aboriginal didgeridoo droning and sean nós singing for example. These styles are easy to define and analyse, each tradition having separate definite musical characteristics. But sometimes it is difficult to say why some music sounds 'Irish' or 'Celtic' as it may not have any obvious defining Irish traditional musical characteristics. The term 'Celtic music' usually reflects a combination of Irish traditional music with various other traditional musics, including those of Scotland and the Shetland Islands; Cape Breton Island, Nova Scotia, Canada; Wales; the Isle of Man; Northumberland in northern England; Brittany, north-west France; and sometimes Galicia in north-western Spain.

One example of a group that uses 'Fusion' is Horslips.

Horslips

Founded in Dublin in 1970.

Members: Jim Lockhart, Barry Devlin, Johnny Fean, Eamon Carr and Charles O'Connor.

Instruments: fiddle, uilleann pipes, whistles, banjo, bodhrán, flutes, mandolin and concertina, and also electric and acoustic guitars, bass guitar, keyboards and drums.

Style: *Celtic Rock*. A fusion of traditional, country, folk and rock styles. Horslips mainly used Irish dance tunes, slow airs and old planxties with a rock interpretation. Many of their albums were based on Irish mythology. They used a mixture of the English and Irish languages in their songs.

'Dearg Donn' and 'King of the Fairies' were number 1 singles. Horslips was a very popular band in the 1970s and toured widely in the USA and Europe.

Instruments in Irish Traditional Music

The core group of traditional instruments used in Irish music are:

- *Irish harp* – pre-tenth century
- *fiddle* – used in Irish music from the seventeenth century
- *uillean pipes* – early eighteenth century
- *flute* – eighteenth century

- *accordion (button and piano)* – twentieth century
- *concertina* – 1850s
- *melodeon* – end of nineteenth century
- *bodhrán*
- *whistles* (tin whistles, low whistles)
- *bones and spoons.*

Non-traditional instruments used nowadays in recordings, concerts and sessions include guitar, banjo, piano, harmonica, bouzouki and many types of synthesised sounds.

Identifying the melody instrument in a traditional musical extract can be difficult at times because sometimes many instruments play just the melodic line, but:

- uillean pipes and their drones are easy to recognise
- listen to recordings of accordions/fiddles, flutes/whistles, guitars/banjos/bouzoukis and try to analyse the **timbre** (tone colour) of each instrument
- in a group session, like a ceili band, you may hear the piano **vamping** or a basic drum kit keeping the beat.

Listen to recordings of some well-known traditional instrumentalists and singers. Try to analyse their style – what type of traditional musical characteristics do they use?

Instrumentalists
Derek Bell (harp); Séamus Ennis, Paddy Maloney, Davy Spillane, Liam O'Floinn, Paddy Keenan (uilleann pipes); Michael Coleman, James Morrison, Frankie Gavin, Paddy Glacken, Mairéad Ní Mhaonaigh (fiddle); Joe Cooley, Sharon Shannon (button accordion); Matt Molloy, Séamus Tansey (flute); Seán Potts, Mary Bergin (tin whistle); Dónal Lunny, Andy Irvine (mandolin / bouzouki).

Singers
Joe Heaney, Tríona Ní Dhomnhaill, Nóirín Ní Riain, Jack MacDhonnacha, Liam O'Mhaonlaí, Paddy Tunney.

Irish Traditional Dances

1   Dance tunes are the most common traditional Irish music played.
2   Most tunes come from the eighteenth and nineteenth centuries.
3   Irish dance forms were influenced by similar European dance forms.
4   Jigs, reels, hornpipes and polkas are the most common dance tunes in the traditional repertoire.
5   Other forms include mazurkas, slides, highlands, barn dances and ceilí dance sets.
6   Rhythm and the internal 'swing' is the most important feature of traditional dance music.

7 Most dance tunes are in a simple repeated form; usually of A (eight-bar phrases) repeated, B repeated. Either or both of these phrases may be repeated again. The tune can then run straight into another dance producing a longer 'set' of dance tunes.

8 Set dances – created by the dancing masters of the eighteenth and nineteenth centuries – are usually set to slow jigs or hornpipe rhythms.

9 Slow airs are often the instrumental rendition of the melodies, or 'airs' of songs, usually sean nós songs.

Table 4.1

Dance Type	Tempo	Time Signature	Origin/Features
Jig Single (slide)	Fast	6/8 (slide also 12/8)	England
Jig Double	Moderately fast	6/8	Second most common Irish dance. Running quaver rhythm.
Jig Slip or hop		9/8	Mixture of note values.
Reel	Fast 2 per bar	2/4 or 4/4	Scotland. Most common Irish dance. Running quavers.
Hornpipe Also Scottische /Highlands	Steady 4 per bar	4/4	England. Accented, dotted rhythm.
Polka	Fast 2 per bar	2/4	Bohemia. Strong rhythm—West Munster set dances.

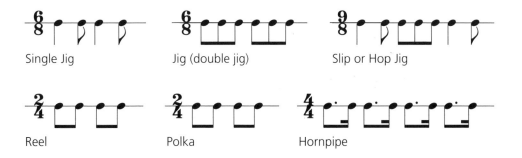

Single Jig   Jig (double jig)   Slip or Hop Jig

Reel   Polka   Hornpipe

The performance of Irish traditional dancing has flourished in the past fifty years. Worldwide appreciation of this art form, which emphasises technique, speed of step and costumes, has increased with national and international Irish dancing competitions. In recent years, Irish music has enjoyed growing popularity worldwide, largely as a result of the wildly successful, internationally performed dance and music stage extravaganza *Riverdance*, as well as the 'steerage scene' from the movie *Titanic*.

The Irish Harp

- There are two types of Irish harp: the ancient Celtic (Gaelic) harp; and the neo-Irish harp.
- *Cruit* or *clairseach* means harp 'as ghaelige'.
- From the fifteenth to the eighteenth century the harp was an aristocratic instrument played by professional harpists.
- Planxty means a piece of music for harp (usually honouring some patron or chieftain).

Table 4.2

Celtic or Gaelic Harp	Neo-Irish Harp
■ 22 strings made of bronze or wire.	■ 34/36 strings made of gut or nylon.
■ Plucked by fingernails.	■ Played with fingertips.
■ Resonant, rich bell-like tone.	■ Softer, gentler tone.
■ Strings need to be dampened.	■ Sound does not vibrate for long.
■ Based on drones in F and G.	■ Tuned in C (diatonic).
■ Tuned approximately in B flat.	■ Invented by John Egan.
■ Made from bogwood.	■ Smaller version of the concert harp but without pedals.
■ Melody played on lower strings by the right hand.	■ Metal levers used to tune harp Melody played in treble by right hand, left hand plays bass.
■ Turlough O'Carolan; Denis Hempson.	■ Laoise Kelly.

5 Understanding Musical Characteristics

This is covered in the Listening Paper I and Composition Paper II.

It is very important to have an understanding of musical analysis and musical terminology used to answer questions in the set works, aural skills and Irish music sections and also in performance and composition. You must be able to comprehend these musical elements and distinguish their features in each question and musical extract:

- cadences
- compositional devices
- dynamics
- form
- harmony
- historical periods
- instrumental techniques
- instrumentation
- key relationship

- melodic shape
- orchestration
- range
- rhythm/metre
- style or genre
- tempo
- texture
- time signature
- tonality.

Some Common Questions

- From which movement is this extract taken?
- What is the tonality of this extract?
- What is the cadence formed at bars ...?
- In which order do the voices enter at bars ...?
- Fill in the missing notes at bars ...
- Name one instrument playing the melody at bar ...
- Describe the melodic figure at bar ...
- Give a musical term for ...
- Briefly describe two characteristics of the composer's style that can be heard in this movement.
- Name two production techniques in this recording.
- Name one instrumental technique in the accompaniment.
- Which of the following rhythmic patterns is played at bars ...?
- State and describe two differences between the two renditions of the themes.
- Name and describe a compositional technique used in this extract.
- Identify three time signatures used in this extract.

Remember:

■ use correct musical terminology in answering all questions
■ *do not* leave any blank spaces
■ use *more than one-word answers*. Try to elaborate with relevant information, if needed.

Exam Technique

Before the exam:

■ use your time effectively
■ systematically work through your complete Set Work and Irish Music notes
■ use your workbook and CD extracts fully
■ practise composition questions from past papers, now available on the State Examinations Commission website (see below)
■ familiarise yourself with the question types and allocation of marks per question (see page 1).

In the exam:

■ follow all instructions on the exam paper
■ attempt the correct number of questions
■ read each question more than once and study the given melody and harmony bars
■ highlight the key words in the question and note the command word (e.g. state and describe (means state and then describe fully), explain, find, suggest, list etc.)
■ allocate your time carefully, especially in the Composition Paper
■ all musical notations that you have written should be correct and as neat as possible. Use a sharp B pencil when composing.

Past examination papers, marking schemes, Chief Examiners' reports, aural tests, syllabuses and any changes in general guidelines are available from the State Examinations Commission website, www.examinations.ie.

The PPMTA (Post Primary Music Teachers' Association) runs excellent revision workshops every year (www.ppmta.ie).

Don't forget to explore www.scoilnet.ie and www.teachnet.ie.

Historical Periods

Orchestra seating chart: baroque period

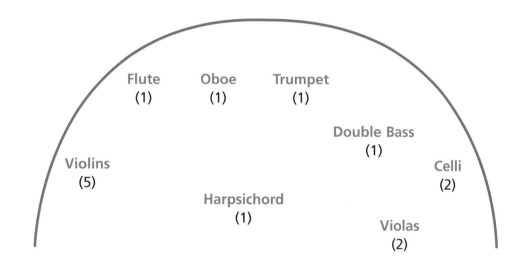

Orchestra seating chart: classical period

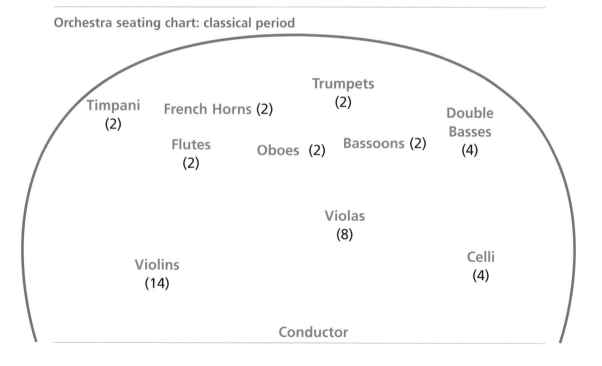

Orchestra seating chart: Romantic period

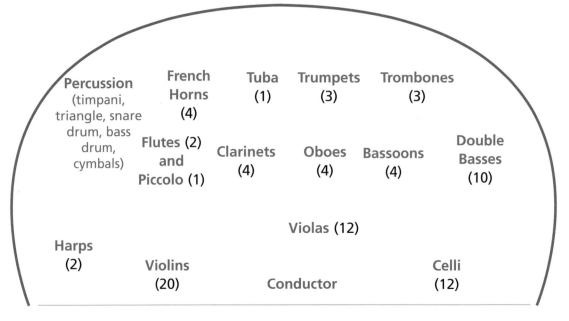

Orchestra seating chart: modern period

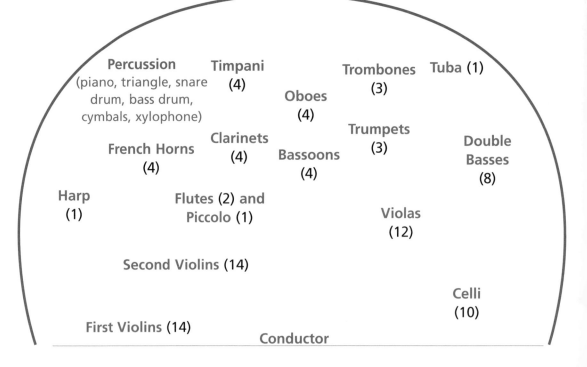

Medieval – c. 800–1400

- use of modes
- monophonic textures – Gregorian chant
- contrasting timbres of medieval instruments
- later more elaborate polyphonic textures – motets
- introduction of harmony.

Renaissance – c. 1450–1600

- rich variety of pieces, both sacred and secular
- mainly vocal forms but also instrumental dances
- more complex textures – four-part vocal counterpoint, lots of imitation
- blending of timbres
- use of modes, but major and minor are more prominent.

Baroque – c.1600–1750

- major/minor key system instigated
- mainly complex polyphonic forms – counterpoint, canon, fugue
- choral music and instrumental dance forms are most important
- figured bass (basso continuo) used in most music
- only one mood per section or piece
- terraced dynamic levels used
- much use of ornamentation in long melodic phrases
- lively, fast rhythms.

Classical – c. 1750–1820

- increase in use of piano and decreased use of harpsichord
- instrumental music forms (symphony, concerto, sonata, string quartet) develop into structured designs
- clear texture (usually homophonic) with melody (short, balanced phrases) and melodic development important
- set number of instrumentalists in organised orchestra.

Romantic – c. 1820–1900

- expansion of the orchestra, development of instruments
- greater technical virtuosity by instrumentalists
- adventurous harmonies with lyrical melodies
- larger contrast in textures, dynamics and timbre
- programme music – more personal compositional styles
- huge variety of pieces and genres – from chamber music and song cycles to huge symphonic works and operas.

Impressionist – c. 1880–1920

■ modal scales (pentatonic, whole tone scales) and unusual harmonies

■ fluid, shifting melodies – no clear-cut form or phrase

■ colourful orchestral timbres.

Modern – c.1900–present

■ huge variety in styles

■ atonal music – serial, electronic, aleatoric music

■ tonal music – neo-classicism, minimalism

■ many iconoclastic composers with their own individual styles

■ huge mixture of instrumental/vocal ensembles

■ fusion with popular, folk, jazz and rock music styles

■ film music and musicals very prominent

■ personalities very important (performers, conductors, composers and orchestras).

Style/Genre

Style describes the characteristic way composers of different eras compose a piece of music: the way the many musical elements of melody, rhythm, harmony, timbre, texture, form, tempo etc. are put together to form a piece of music, whether a baroque chorale or a modern film score.

What words can you use to describe the 'style' or 'genre' of a given extract?

■ classical

■ vocal

■ operatic

■ symphonic

■ instrumental

■ popular

■ rock

■ folk

■ traditional

■ blues

■ electronic music

■ ethnic

■ non-Western

■ jazz/jazzy

■ programme music

■ film music

■ absolute music

■ fusion

■ musical

■ Oriental

■ secular

■ sacred.

> **Hint**
>
> Listen to as many musical styles as possible. Try to label each piece of music you hear with a stylistic description.

Dynamics

Dynamics means the loudness or quietness of a sound. You must interpret each dynamic marking depending on:

- comparison with other dynamics in the music
- the dynamic range for that instrument or ensemble
- the ability of the performer(s).

Traditionally, dynamic markings are based on Italian words.

Typical Dynamic Markings

ppp   pp   p   mp   mf   f   ff   fff

p = piano, soft   *m* = mezzo, moderately   *f* = forte, loud

If the composer wants the change from one dynamic level to another to be gradual, different markings are added. A *crescendo* (cresc.) means 'gradually get louder'; a *decrescendo* or *diminuendo* (dim.) means 'gradually get softer'. These markings also mean *crescendo* and *diminuendo*:

crescendo   *diminuendo*

General rule

Each dynamic level that is louder or softer than the previous level should be twice as loud or soft: *ff* should be approximately twice as loud as *f*.

Hints

- In *melody composition* you must insert appropriate dynamic markings for the entire 16-bar melody (or 8-bar at Ordinary Level), not just for your own written 12 bars.
- In much music, the dynamics decrease at the cadence point (especially at a suspension/resolution) but a strong, final perfect cadence may be loud to very loud.
- When inputting dynamics, it is sometimes useful to follow the shape of the melodic line, especially at the climax: a crescendo is easier to play with an ascending motion than a descending scale, for example.
- There is no need to insert dynamics in every bar – one, two or three markings per phrase is more than enough.

A *cresc.* or *dim.* hairpin must be preceded by an appropriate dynamic marking. The *cresc.* or *dim.* hairpin must then go to another appropriate dynamic level.

Dynamics – Instrument Ranges

When inserting dynamics for your melody, be careful of using dynamic levels that are nearly impossible to play on certain instruments. For example: an *fff* marking for a flute playing its lowest notes or a *pp* marking for a very high trumpet opening is inappropriate as it is nearly impossible to play well. So:

■ learn the ranges of instruments/voices (*tessitura*)
■ use comfortable dynamic markings (*pp* to *ff*) in your melody composition.

Articulation

Articulation is how one sings or plays the notes of a piece. Exactly how each articulation should be played depends on the instrument playing it, as well as on the style and period of the music.

Accents are markings that are used to indicate especially strong-sounding notes with a definite attack. Some accents may even be played by making the note longer or more separate from the other notes, rather than just louder. The exact performance of each type of accent depends on the instrument and the style and period of the music, but the *sforzando (sfz)* and *fortepiano (fp)*-type accents are usually louder and longer, and more likely to be used in a long note that starts loudly and then suddenly gets much softer.

■ *Staccato* – short, detached notes. Dot under or over the note only.
■ *Marcato* – stressed, accented notes.
■ *Legato* – the opposite of staccato. Smooth, connected series of notes (varies in string or wind playing).
■ *Slur* – only the first note of a set of slurred notes has a definite articulation. All other notes under the slur are played *legato*.
■ *No articulation marking* – Much music has little or no articulation marking. Notes can be played separated or, more commonly, it is up to the performer to interpret the music in a correct stylistic manner.

> Phrase marks and/or articulation markings are needed for the *melody composition* question. If using articulation marks, make sure you understand how your markings will affect the performance of the piece by the instrument that you chose.

Tempo

The **tempo** of a piece of music is the speed at which it is played.

There are two ways to specify a tempo:

- **Metronome markings** are absolute and specific.
- **Verbal descriptions** are more relative and subjective.

Metronome markings are given in beats per minute. Tempo instructions are usually given in Italian.

Some common tempo markings:

- *grave* – very slow and solemn
- *largo* – slow and broad
- *larghetto* – not quite as slow as largo
- *adagio* – slow
- *lento* – slow
- *andante* – literally 'walking', a medium slow tempo
- *moderato* – moderate, or medium
- *allegretto* – not as fast as allegro
- *allegro* – fast
- *vivo* or *vivace* – lively and brisk
- *presto* – very fast
- *prestissimo* – very, very fast.

More useful Italian terms:

- *poco* – a little
- *molto* – a lot
- *più* – more
- *meno* – less
- *mosso* – literally 'moved'; movement
- *rallentando (rall.)* or *ritardando (rit.)* – slow down
- *accelerando (accel.)* – speed up.

Texture

When you describe the texture of a piece of music, you are describing how much is going on in the music at any given moment. For example, the texture of a piece of music may have many or just one or two layers. It might be made up of rhythm alone, or of a melody line with chordal accompaniment, or many interweaving melodies.

Terms that describe texture:

- dense/rich
- thin/sparse
- monophonic or monophony
- homophonic or homophony
- polyphonic or polyphony
- counterpoint
- contrapuntal

- countermelody
- descant
- canon or canonic
- fugue or fugal
- stretto
- heterophony
- antiphonal.

Monophonic music has only one melodic line, with no harmony or counterpoint. There may be rhythmic accompaniment, but only one line that has specific pitches; plainchant is one example.

Homophonic music has one clearly melodic line; it is the most important line musically. All other parts provide accompaniment of one type or another. There may be some melodic interest in the accompaniment parts but it is clear that they are not independent melodic parts, either because they have the same rhythm as the melody (i.e. are not independent) or because their main purpose is to fill in the chords or harmony (i.e. they are not really melodies).

Polyphonic music can also be called counterpoint, or contrapuntal music. If more than one independent melody is occurring at the same time, the music is polyphonic.

Examples of polyphonic music:
- rounds, canons, and fugues. (Even if there is only one melody, if different people are singing or playing it at different times, the parts sound independent.)
- much baroque music is contrapuntal (e.g. parts of the Aria Duet in J. S. Bach's Cantata BWV 78).
- most music for large instrumental groups such as bands or orchestras is contrapuntal at least some of the time
- music that is mostly homophonic can become temporarily polyphonic if an independent countermelody is added.

Musical textures

Monophony

Polyphony

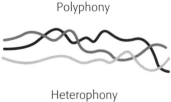

Homophony

Heterophony

Cadences

A cadence is a place in a piece of music that feels like a stopping or resting point. It is made up of two chords (sometimes with an approach chord). There are four types of cadence, depending on what chord progressions are used.

Cadences end phrases or sections of music and so the form/structure of a piece is closely linked to cadential points. Most tonal pieces use regularly spaced cadences (and phrasing) in a 4–8–16–32-bar pattern.

> **Hint**
>
> When trying to identify cadences in a listening extract, ask yourself:
> 1 Does it sound *finished* or *unfinished*?
> 2 Does it end in a major or minor chord?
> 3 Is it a strong ending or a weak ending?
> 4 Does the music feel unresolved (i.e. as though it needs to carry on)?

Changes in the rhythm of a piece, a pause in the rhythm, a lengthening of the note values or a slowing of the harmonic rhythm are often found at cadence points.

Table 5.1 Cadences

Name	Major Key	Minor Key
Perfect Cadence Strong final sound	V—I Use in root position at end of piece	V—i Chord V always has accidental in minor key
Plagal Cadence Sounds like *A-men* at the end of a hymn	IV—I	iv—I Minor to minor
Imperfect Cadence Ends on dominant chord	I or ii or IV—V	I or iv—V
Interrupted Cadence Tonality change — unexpected sound	V—vi Major to minor chord in a major key	V—VI Major to major chord in a minor key

Intervals

An interval is the distance between two pitches. The name of an interval depends both on how the notes are written and the actual distance between the notes as measured in semitones.

The first step in naming the interval is to find the distance between the notes *as they are written on the stave*. For example, the interval between G and C is a fourth; the interval between F and E is a seventh. **Compound intervals** are larger than an octave.

Perfect Intervals

Unison, octaves, fourths and fifths can be perfect intervals:

Perfect intervals

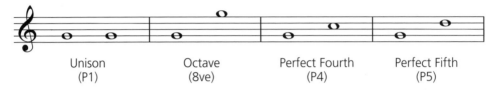

Unison	Octave	Perfect Fourth	Perfect Fifth
(P1)	(8ve)	(P4)	(P5)

Major and Minor Intervals

Seconds, thirds, sixths, and sevenths can be major intervals or minor intervals. The minor interval is always a semitone smaller than the major interval.

- 1 semitone = minor second (m2)
- 2 semitones = major second (M2)
- 3 semitones = minor third (m3)
- 4 semitones = major third (M3)
- 8 semitones= minor sixth (m6)
- 9 semitones = major sixth (M6)
- 10 semitones = minor seventh (m7)
- 11 semitones = major seventh (M7)
- 12 semitones = perfect octave (P8)

Major and minor intervals

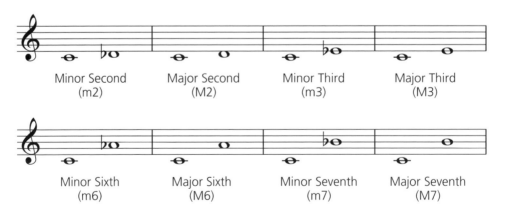

Minor Second	Major Second	Minor Third	Major Third
(m2)	(M2)	(m3)	(M3)

Minor Sixth	Major Sixth	Minor Seventh	Major Seventh
(m6)	(M6)	(m7)	(M7)

Augmented and Diminished Intervals

If an interval is a semitone larger than a perfect or a major interval, it is called **augmented**. An interval that is a semitone smaller than a perfect or a minor interval is called **diminished**.

Augmented and diminished intervals

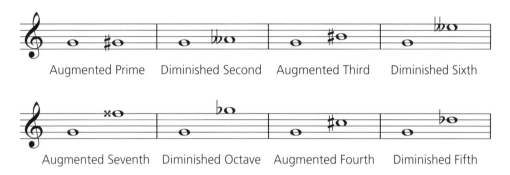

Augmented Prime   Diminished Second   Augmented Third   Diminished Sixth

Augmented Seventh   Diminished Octave   Augmented Fourth   Diminished Fifth

A diminished fifth and an augmented fourth are both six semitones, or **three whole tones**, so another term for this interval is a **tritone**.

Consonance and Dissonance

Notes that sound good together when played at the same time are called **consonant**. Notes that are **dissonant** can sound harsh or unpleasant when played at the same time. Or they may feel 'unstable'; if you hear a chord with a dissonance in it, you may feel that the music is pulling you towards the chord that **resolves** the dissonance. In music certain combinations are consonant and others dissonant. Consonance and dissonance can refer to both chords and intervals.

The simple intervals that are considered to be consonant are the minor third, major third, perfect fourth, perfect fifth, minor sixth, major sixth, and the octave.

Chords that contain only these intervals are considered to be 'stable', restful chords that don't need to be resolved.

The intervals considered to be **dissonant** are the minor second, the major second, the minor seventh, the major seventh, and particularly the tritone.

These intervals are all considered to be tension-producing. In tonal music, chords containing dissonances are considered 'unstable'; when we hear them, we expect them to move on to a more stable chord. Moving from a dissonance to the consonance that is expected to follow it is called **resolution**.

The pattern of tension and release created by resolved dissonances is part of what makes a piece of music exciting and interesting.

Resolving dissonances

Rhythm

- The term **rhythm** as used by musicians can refer to many things. It can mean the basic, repetitive pulse of the music or a rhythmic pattern that is repeated throughout the music. It can also refer to the pattern of note values.
- The **beat** is the steady pulse in the music. Anything that happens at the same time as a strong pulse is 'on the beat'; anything that happens at any other time is 'off the beat' (syncopation).
- Measure or **bar**. Beats are grouped into measures or bars. The first beat is usually the strongest, and in most music, most of the bars have the same number of beats. This sets up a basic rhythm in the pulse of the music.
- **Syncopation** occurs when a strong note happens either on a weak beat or off the beat.

Some words to describe **rhythmic features** in a Listening Paper question:

- syncopated
- dotted
- complex
- simple
- strict/steady
- polyrhythm
- ostinato
- waltz-like
- triplet
- free rhythm
- rubato
- back beat
- hemiola.

Time Signatures

The **time signature** tells you the metre of the music by defining both the number of beats in a bar and the type of note value (minims, crotchets, quavers) that fills one beat.

The **metre** of a piece of music is its basic **pulse**; the time signature is the symbol that tells you the metre of the piece.

Beats and Measures

In most music, things tend to happen right at the beginning of each beat. This is called being on the **downbeat**.

Clef, key signature and time signature

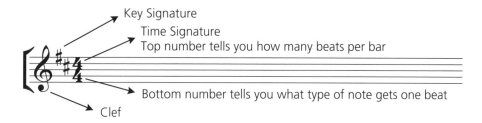

The **time signature** appears at the beginning of a piece of music, after the key signature. Only one time signature needs to be inserted in Questions 1–3 melody writing. Unlike the key signature, *do not* insert the time signature at the start of every stave/phrase (unless you are changing time signature – which there is no need for you to do).

Reading Time Signatures

Most time signatures contain two numbers. The top number tells you how many beats there are in a measure. The bottom number tells you what kind of note gets a beat. A few time signatures don't have to be written as numbers. 4/4 time is used so much that it is often called **common time**, written as a **C**.

Key Signature

The **key signature** is a list of all the sharps and flats in the key that the music is in.

The sharps or flats always appear in the **same order** in all key signatures.

Order of sharps and flats

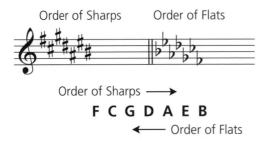

Order of Sharps   Order of Flats

Order of Sharps ⟶

F C G D A E B

⟵ Order of Flats

The key signature at the beginning of a musical stave lists the sharps or flats in the key. The key signature comes right after the clef symbols on particular lines or spaces, or some flat symbols. If there are no flats or sharps listed after the clef symbol, then the key signature is that all notes are natural.

Hint

If you do not know what key you are in, the key signature can help you find out. If you are in a major key: if the key contains sharps, the name of the key (doh or tonic key) is *one semitone higher than the last sharp* in the key signature; if the key contains flats, the name of the key signature (doh or tonic key) is the name of the *second-to-last flat* in the key signature.

- Clef and key signature are the only symbols that must appear on every stave. The key signature tells you whether the note is sharp, flat or natural.

- In the diagram of the key signatures you will see that sharps and flats are always added in the same order as keys get sharper or flatter. The order of flats and sharps, like the order of the keys themselves, follows a **circle of fifths.**

C major and F major

C major   F major

The only major keys that these rules do not work for are C major (no flats or sharps) and F major (one flat). It is easiest just to memorise the key signatures for these two very common keys.

Key signatures

If the music is in a *minor* key, it will be in the *relative minor* of the major key for that key signature. If you cannot tell from the sound of the music whether you are in a major or minor key, the best clue is to look at the final chord and for any accidental in the given music.

A **relative minor** is always three semitones lower than its relative major.

The **harmonic minor scale** raises the seventh note of the scale by one half step, whether you are going up or down the scale.

In the **melodic minor scale**, the sixth and seventh notes of the scale are each raised by one half step when going up the scale and are flattened (naturalised) when going back down a scale. You must use this type of minor when composing melodies.

6 Melody

Words that describe the shape or contour of a melody:

- repeated notes
- stepwise motion
- interval leaps
- ascending
- descending
- triadic
- arpeggio
- countermelody
- descant.

A **melody** is a series of notes, one after another.

Melodic Phrases

Melodies are often described as being made up of phrases.

A melodic phrase is a group of notes that make sense together and express a definite melodic 'idea', but it takes more than one phrase to make a complete melody.

How do you spot a phrase in a melody? The melody usually pauses slightly at the end of each phrase (cadence point).

In vocal music, the musical phrases tend to follow the phrases and sentences of the text.

Melody Writing

Paper II, Question 1, 2 or 3. Answer *one* melody composition question.

Use a sharp B pencil and be as neat in your notation as possible.

First of all, identify which question you want to answer. Study the given phrase and decide which instrument is most suitable for this melody:

- see which instruments are provided
- look at the clef
- look at the range of the given material.

Write for a flexible instrument, such as a clarinet or violin (if in treble clef). These instruments both have a wide range and can effortlessly play all styles of music.

Then:

- check both the key signature and the given phrase to decide the tonic key (be aware of the harmonic outline of the given bars and look out for accidentals which may mean that the piece is in a minor key).
- write out your triad scale for this key (or sol-fa).

You may wish to use the rough work manuscript before transferring the final melody. In any case, double-check every bar of your answer when you are finished.

- Draw out your twelve barlines, double bar, clef and key signature, if needed.
- Try to keep four bars of music to each line of stave, as in the given music.
- Number each bar or number the first bar on each stave.
- Be careful of upbeats (anacrusis) – don't forget to fill in any missing upbeat from the end of the fourth bar.
- With an upbeat melody, remember to subtract that value from the final (sixteenth) bar from the time signature.
- Fill in the structural phrase marks or breathing commas – this helps you to visualise the shape of your melody better.
- Whether using tonic sol-fa or plotting chord progressions, fill in the final cadence and the other two cadences at bars 7–8 (modulation – perfect) and 11–12 (imperfect).
- Remember your modulation (if needed).
- Don't forget to mark in sequence (bars 9–11) and climax (bars 13–16) lightly in pencil so you remember these compositional techniques when you come to notate the melody.
- If writing a melody plotting chords, insert chord names lightly over each bar.
- Plot out the rhythm for the full piece:
  1 Develop the first phrases' rhythmic ideas in the A1 and A2 phrases. Bars 5 and 13 should aurally (and subconsciously) be somewhat similar to bar 1 by developing the rhythm and melody from bar 1. This reinforces the tight structure of the overall melody.
  2 If using A A1 B A2 form, find an interesting motif from phrase 1 to use as an ascending or descending sequence in the B (bars 9–12) phrase. A scale-like passage or simple interval jumps is usual. Be careful that the sequence is not aimless and makes melodic sense. Do *not* use rhythmic ideas that are completely out of style with the remainder of the melody.
- Write your melody – it must be musically and stylistically sound and interesting.
- Phrase 4 must be the climax of the piece. Extend the range upwards (noting the instruments' capabilities) and end in a strong perfect cadence. End on a longer note value.

- In *Question 3*, the rhythm must be developed in the given style, as it is a dance form.

    1   Be careful of the metre/time signature, especially in compound time: 6/8.

    2   Be aware of the anacrusis (upbeat).

- In *Question 2*, the setting of text to music, the rhythm and structure of your melody must come from the word setting and the syllable structure. Read through the given text many times before you decide on your time signature and then on your rhythmic/syllabic structure.

- In a minor key be aware of the augmented second interval between the sixth and raised seventh notes (harmonic minor) of the scale. In an ascending scale sharpen each sixth and seventh note. Naturalise each note in a descending scale passage (melodic minor).

Modulation

In a major key the usual modulation is to the dominant (chord V of the tonic or soh). In a minor key, modulate to the relative major (the major key signature of the piece). Modulations can occur at the end of the second or third phrase. Return back to the tonic (doh) for the ending of your melody.

Don't forget to add (if necessary):

- tempo markings
- dynamic markings
- expression markings
- phrasing and /or articulation.

Common Errors

- No marks will be awarded for *exact* repetition of given material or material that is much too similar in rhythm or melody to the notes written.
- Incorrect modulations, especially inaccuracy in accidentals, is common.
- No feeling of phrase, structure and cadence points.
- Poor layout and messy notation.
- Missing anacrusis (upbeat) from each phrase and last bar rhythm incorrect.

Marking Scheme

Grade A
Excellent melodic style and structure. Good points of climax, convincing rhythm and development of opening ideas (good, convincing rhythm/text development).

Marks: 34–40.

Grade B
Very aware of shape and structure; musical, with good points of climax. Well-developed opening ideas (dance style maintained/good text setting).

Marks: 28–33.

Grade C
Good sense of melodic and rhythmic interest. (Fairly well-maintained rhythmic dance style/careful text setting.)

Marks: 22–27.

Grade D
Careful melody and shape. Reasonable shape and accurate rhythm (accurate word setting).

Marks: 16–21.

Grade E
Little melodic interest, some inaccurate rhythms (some inaccuracies in word setting).

Marks: 10–15.

Grade F
No sense of key, inconsistent rhythm, poor structure (inconsistent word setting, poor shape).

Marks: 0–9.

Deductions, if omitted or deficient: modulation at a suitable point (4); phrasing (structural, articulation or both), dynamics, instrument (up to 2 each). Accept one correct instrument only (clef and range).

7 Harmony

Harmony is the relationship of any notes that happen at the same time.

Major and Minor Chords

- The most commonly used triads form major chords and minor chords.
- All major and minor chords have an interval of a perfect fifth between the root and the fifth of the chord.
- If the interval between the root and the third of the chord is a major third the triad is a major chord.
- If the interval between the root and the third of the chord is a minor third the triad is a minor chord.

Major and minor chords

In major chords, the third of the chord is a major third above the root.

In both major and minor chords, the fifth of the chord is a perfect fifth above the root.

In minor chords, the third of the chord is a minor third above the root.

Augmented and Diminished Chords

Because they don't contain a perfect fifth, augmented and diminished chords have an unsettled feeling and are normally used sparingly.

Chord progressions

Here are some good chord progressions that you can use in Paper II:

- chord ii usually goes to V
  I – vi – IV – ii – V or I – IV – ii – V
  but chord V rarely goes to chord ii
- V can go to I, vi or IV
- chord vi usually goes either to chord IV or chord ii.

Harmonic Textures

- **Implied harmony**. A melody all by itself (**monophony**) can have an implied harmony, even if no other notes are sounding at the same time. In melody writing (Questions 1–3, Paper II) construct a melody so that it strongly suggests a harmony that could accompany it.
- **Drones**. The simplest way to add harmony to a melody is to play it with drones. A drone is a note that changes rarely or not at all.
- **Parallel harmony** occurs when different lines in the music go up or down together (usually following the melody).
- **Homophony** is a texture of music in which there is one line that is obviously the melody. The rest of the notes are harmony and accompaniment.

Harmonic Analysis

Harmonic analysis simply means understanding how a chord is related to the key and to the other chords in a piece of music.

- **Harmonic rhythm** refers to how often the chords change.
- **Diatonic** harmony stays in a particular major or minor key.
- **Chromatic** harmony includes notes and chords that are not in the key and so contains many accidentals.
- **Dissonance** refers to a note, chord or interval that does not fit into the triadic. A dissonance may sound surprising, jarring, even disagreeable.

Accompaniment

- All the parts of the music that are not melody are part of the **accompaniment**. This includes rhythmic parts, harmonies, the bass line, and chords.
- The **bass line** is the string of notes that are the lowest notes being sung or played. The bass line also often outlines the chord progression, and it is often the most noticeable line of the accompaniment.
- **Inner voices** are accompaniment parts that fill in the music between the melody (which is often the highest part) and the bass line.
- **Descant**: the melody is not always the highest line in the music. Attention is naturally drawn to high notes, so a part that is higher than the melody is sometimes given a special name such as 'descant'.

Basic Triads in a Major Key

The most likely chords to show up in a key are the chords that you can make in that key without using accidentals. So these chords have both names and numbers that tell how they fit into the key.

The chords are numbered using Roman numerals from I to vii.

- To find all the basic chords in a key, build a simple triad (in the key) on each note of the scale. You'll find that although the chords change from one key to the next, the *pattern* of major and minor chords is always the same.
- Capital Roman numerals are used for major chords and small Roman numerals for minor chords .
- In a major key, the chords built on the first, fourth, and fifth degrees of the scale are always major chords (I, IV, and V). The chords built on the second, third, and sixth degrees of the scale are always minor chords (ii, iii, and vi). The chord built on the seventh degree of the scale is a diminished chord.

A Hierarchy of Chords

In most music, the most common chord is I. It is the tonal centre of the music. IV and V (or V^7) are also likely to be very common.

Naming Harmonic Relationships

In classical music another set of names for chords (and their harmonic relationships) and degrees of the scale is commonly used.

> I = tonic
> ii = supertonic
> iii = mediant
> IV = subdominant
> V = dominant
> vi = submediant
> vii = leading note

Modulation

Sometimes a piece of music moves into a new key. This is called modulation. It is very common in traditional classical music; longer movements almost always spend at least some time in a different key (usually a closely related key such as the *dominant* or the *relative minor* or *relative major*).

Triads in Root Position

Chords in **root position** are the most basic way to write a triad. In root position, the root, which is the note that names the chord, is the lowest note. The simplest way to write a triad is as a stack of thirds, in root position.

First and Second Inversions

Three triads of C major

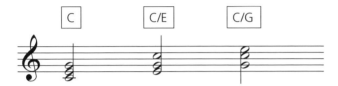

If the third of the chord is the lowest note, the chord is in first inversion. If the fifth of the chord is the lowest note, the chord is in second inversion. It does not matter how far away the higher notes are, or how many of each note there are, all that matters is **which note is lowest**.

- **C** is a chord **I** of C and has C as its first lowest note (root position chord).
- **C/E** is a chord **Ib** of C with E as its first lowest note (first inversion). Do not overuse this type of chord as it is a weaker-sounding chord than a root position chord, but it does work very well in an ascending or descending progression: **C, G/b, am, G, dm/f, G7, C.**
- **C/G** is a chord **Ic** of C with G as its first lowest note (second inversion). This type of second inversion chord only works well at a Ic – V – I cadence point.

Treble Clef and Bass Clef

Treble clef and bass clef

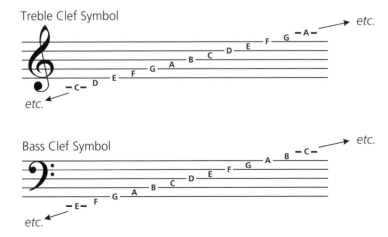

The clef symbol on a music stave tells you which pitches belong on the lines and spaces of that stave.

The first symbol that appears at the beginning of every stave is a clef symbol. It tells you which note (A, B, C, D, E, F or G) goes on each line or space. The other notes are arranged on the stave so that the next letter is always on the next higher line or space.

Alto clef and tenor clef

Most music these days is written in either bass clef or treble clef, but some music is written in the **alto** or tenor clef. Whatever line it centres on is middle C. Music is easier to read and write if most of the notes fall on the stave and few ledger lines have to be used. Instruments with ranges that do not fall comfortably into either bass or treble clef may use a C clef or may be transposing instruments.

A very small '8' at the bottom of the treble clef symbol means that the notes should sound one octave lower than they are written.

Harmony in the Exam

Paper II, Question 4, 5 or 6. Answer *one* harmony question.

This section is worth 60 marks, or 15% of your overall music exam.

It is therefore vital that you understand how to:

■ identify cadence points
■ harmonise correctly
■ notate in the bass clef
■ use chord inversions.

Use a sharp B pencil and be as neat in your notation as possible. Don't forget to fill out the chord box or the scale with triads. Ordinary Level candidates must fill these out for marks. First of all:

- identify which question you want to answer (Question 5 is the most popular choice)
- study the given material in each question
- look at the chord box to check the tonic key
- plot your chords in the chord box and/or write out your triad scale for this key
- don't forget you need an '*m*' sign for a minor chord if using chord symbols (chords ii and vi in a major key and chords i and iv in a minor key)
- in a key with flats or sharps, you *must* use the flat or sharp symbol beside the chord name if needed.

In all harmony questions:

- be alert to given material with an anacrusis (upbeat) – in the final bar, subtract the value of the upbeat from the time signature
- try to find the cadence points. Find the harmonic outline of the given bars and structural phrasing of the piece (Questions 5 and 6) – this helps you to plot the chord progressions of any cadences
- remember: there may be a modulation in any of the questions. Treat it the same way as you would for your melody-writing question.

Question 4

The melody and rhythm must be developed in the *given* style. This is a good question to attempt if you are good at melody writing.

- First, identify cadence points from the chords provided.
- Start by filling out your bass notes in the given style. Keep the bass simple, but don't use long note values in every bar.
- Write your melody – it must be musically and stylistically sound and interesting.
- Be careful of doubling any of the notes of the chord, but be especially careful not to double the third of the chord between the melody and bass notes.
- Try to use the root and third, root and fifth, third and fifth together. This produces better harmony (and better marks) than doubling the root etc. every time you get a root position chord.
- Do *not* use rhythmic ideas that are completely out of style with the given material. Be careful with your rhythms in every time signature, especially if there is an anacrusis (upbeat).
- In a minor key – be aware of the augmented second interval between the sixth and raised seventh notes (harmonic minor) of the scale. In an ascending scale sharpened each sixth and seventh note. Naturalise each note in a descending scale passage (melodic minor).

Question 5
■   First try to identify the cadence points from the given melody (insert a square bracket over the two empty boxes that you believe is a cadence).
■   Look out for a modulation within the melody (accidentals in the melody) and work accordingly.
■   Study the melody (every note, not just the first note of the bar) under each chord box and decide which chords may suit.
■   Write the chord (choices of chords) above the empty box until you are happy with the overall chord progressions in that phrase. Be aware of passing notes in each bar and suspension/resolution notes at cadence points.
■   Try to use some first inversion chords if you feel they would fit the progression.
■   Fill out the empty chord boxes neatly and accurately.
■   From your chords, fill in the bass notes using a development of the given style. Be aware of patterns where first inversion chords may fit. Use root position bass notes at cadence points.
■   Double-check every bar when finished for accurate notation of rhythms and chords symbols.

Question 6
■   First try to identify the cadence points from the given melody (insert a square bracket over the two empty boxes that you believe is a cadence).
■   Look out for a modulation within the melody (accidentals in the melody) and work accordingly.
■   Study the lower melody (every note under the empty chord box, not just the first) under each chord box and decide which chords may suit.
■   Write the chord (choices of chords) above the empty box until you are happy with the overall chord progressions in that phrase. Be aware of passing notes in each bar and suspension/resolution notes at cadence points.
■   Try to use some first inversion chords if you feel they would fit the progression.
■   Fill out the empty chord boxes neatly and accurately.
■   When writing the descant or countermelody, remember:
    1   keep the range of the descant higher than the lower given melody
    2   the melody and rhythm must be developed in the given style and must be musically and stylistically sound and interesting
    3   be careful of doubling any of the notes of the chord, but be especially careful not to double the third of the chord between the descant and given melody notes
    4   try to use the root and third, root and fifth, third and fifth together. This produces better harmony (and better marks) than doubling the root etc. every time you get a root position chord.
■   Use contrary motion as a melodic device; also look out for passages where you could use some canonic material.

■ When there is a more complex bar of rhythm in the given melody, you use longer note values in that bar and visa versa.

> You do *not* need to add:
> ■ tempo markings
> ■ dynamic markings
> ■ expression markings
> ■ phrasing and /or articulation.
> You do not need to use chord iii and chord vii.

Double-check every bar of your answer when you have finished.

> **Common Errors**
>
> ■ In Questions 4 and 6, no marks will be awarded for *exact* repetition of given material or material that is much too similar in rhythm or melody notes written. Develop the melody and/or descant in the given style.
> ■ Incorrect chords at cadence points lose valuable marks.
> ■ Poor layout and messy notation will not help you gain marks.
> ■ Inaccurate bass clef notation is common.
> ■ Inaccurate bass clef (lower part) rhythms are common.
> ■ Boring, long-value bass clef notes (semibreves, minims) throughout Questions 5 and 6 lose marks if not in the given style of the opening few bars. Don't be *too* adventurous, though!

Typical Marking Scheme

Question 4
Adding melody and bass notes from a set of chords.

Bass: 1 mark per correct bass note under each chord symbol if treble melody note is also correct: 1 x 20 = approx. 20 marks.

Quality of bass line: approx. 5 marks.

Melody: approx. 35 marks, as follows:

Grade A
Excellent melodic style and structure. Good points of climax, convincing rhythm and development of opening ideas.

Marks: 30–35.

Grade B
Very aware of shape and structure, musical with good points of climax. Well developed opening ideas.

Marks: 24–29.

Grade C
Good sense of melodic and rhythmic interest.

Marks: 18–23.

Grade D
Careful melody and shape. Reasonable shape and accurate rhythm.

Marks: 13–17.

Grade E
Little melodic interest, some inaccurate rhythms.

Marks: 8–12.

Grade F
No sense of key, inconsistent rhythm, poor structure.

Marks: 0–7.

Question 5
Adding bass notes and chord indications at cadences.

Chords: 1 mark per correct chord that fits.

Quality of Overall Chord Progressions: no marks for chord if suffix omitted/minor chords not indicated or accidentally omitted. Dominant and Dominant seventh may be used in adjacent boxes.

Bass: 1 mark per correct note for every correct chord.

Quality of Bass Line (including note placement): up to 2 marks.

Question 6
Adding descant notes and chord indications at cadence points

Chords: 1 mark per correct chord that fits. (Bass notes need not be indicated.)

Descant: up to 40 marks allocated as above (Question 4).

Triads

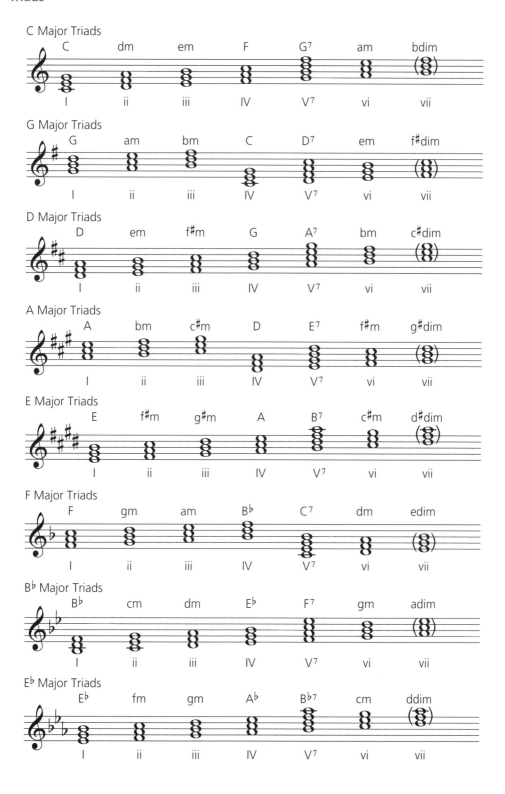

8 Set Works

Score Reading

Score reading your set works can be difficult to achieve when studying alone. Use group work (two or three students) to improve your active listening: by asking each other questions about the themes and musical characteristics; by stopping the CD to make sure everyone is at that particular bar number; and by each student following a different instrument or family of instruments in the score.

- Check through the score, marking in musical terms and symbols and abbreviations for the instruments.
- Be aware of repeat signs and symbols that mean the music will go back to the start or to the sign or coda, etc.
- Check the time signature and tempo marking of each section.
- Always listen out for unusual features or easily recognisable instruments at certain points of the score. These pointers will help you if you get lost.
- At first, follow the score with your fingertips and your foot tapping out the pulse. Match what you hear with what you see.
- Be careful of following a score when the amount of systems per page changes (the two slanting black parallel lines between systems).

Set Works: Group A

(To be examined in 2005–2007.)

- J. S. Bach, Cantata BWV 78, 'Jesu, der du meine Seele' (1724)
- P. I. Tchaikovsky, *Romeo and Juliet Fantasy Overture* (1880)
- Queen, 'Bohemian Rhapsody' (1975)
- Gerald Barry, Piano Quartet No. 1 (1992)

Quick Revision – Set Works A

Table 8.1

Work	Movement/ Section	Time Signature	Key Signature	Style	Tempo
J.S. Bach (1685–1750) Cantata BWV 78 'Jesu, der du meine Seele' (1724)	Chorus SATB	3/4	Gm	Baroque sacred cantata for the fourteenth Sunday after Trinity, based on text by Johann Rist	No tempo markings
	Aria (Duet) Soprano and Alto	4/4	B$\flat$		
	Recitativo Tenor	C	Gm C		
	Aria Tenor	6/8	Gm		
	Recitativo Bass	C	E$\flat$ A$\flat$ Fm		Vivace Adagio Andante
	Aria Bass	C	Cm		No tempo markings
	Chorale Chorus SATB	C	Gm: ends in G		
P.I. Tchaikovsky (1840–93) *Romeo and Juliet*	Introduction	C	F#m Fm/A$\flat$ Am	Romantic symphonic fantasy overture	Andante non tasto quasi moderato
	Exposition		Bm		Allegro guisto
	Development				
	Recapitulation				
	Coda	B			Moderato assai
Queen 'Bohemian Rhapsody'	Intro	4/4	B$\flat$	Pop close harmony style	Slowly
		5/4			
	Song	4/4	B$\flat$–E$\flat$	Rock ballad	
		2/4			
	Opera	4/4	A–E$\flat$	Pastiche – popular operatic section	Twice as fast ♪=♩
		2/4			
	Song	4/4	E$\flat$	Rock style	
		2/4			
	Coda	4/4	Ends in F		Tempo 1

Work	Movement/ Section	Time Signature	Key Signature	Style	Tempo
Gerald Barry Piano Quartet No 1	A *Si Bheag, Si Mhór*	3/4 4/4		Contemporary classical piano quartet with some trad Irish influences	♩. = 108
	B	3/4, 3/8, 4/4, 2/4, 2/8, 5/8, 3/16			♩. = 72 ♩. = 80 (B2)
	C	3/4, 3/8, 2/8, 3/16, 2/4, 4/4			from ♩ = 58 to ♩ = 168
	D	1/8, 3/16, 2/8, 3/8, 5/16, 3/4, 4/4, 2/4			♩ = 126 wild!
	E	3/4, 3/8, 2/8, 3/16, 4/4, 2/4, 2/8			♩ = 138 (E2)
	F	3/2, 3/4, 4/2, 3/8, 2/2			♩ = 138
	G	2/8, 3/16, 3/8, 2/4, 1/4,			♩ = 126
	H *Lord Mayo's Delight*	2/2, 3/4, 3/2, 3/8			♩ = 104

Revision of Families of Instruments

Table 8.2   Instruments used in Set Works A

Composer	Vocal	Strings	Woodwind	Brass	Percussion	Keyboard/ Other
Bach	✗	✗	✗	✗		✗
Tchaikovsky		✗	✗	✗	✗	
Queen	✗				✗	✗
Barry		✗				✗

Listening Paper I – Recognition of instruments is always tested in the exam. Knowing what instruments are used in each set work and in each section of each set work is a great basis for beginning your complete analytical understanding of the questions that will appear on Paper I.

Knowing what instruments are *not* used in certain sections is also useful as an exam technique.

In the months preceding your exam, you should listen to all your set works *at least* ten times in your own study or revision time (group work is very much recommended when listening in an active way). It is the only way to get to understand and appreciate each set work fully.

CD recordings of most Leaving Certificate Set Works are available from your local music shop, or ask your teacher.

J. S. Bach: 'Jesu, der du meine Seele'

You should:
1   Be able to identify themes and movements from a listening or written extract.
2   Be able to identify instruments and voices in each movement from a listening or written extract.
3   Understand the compositional and instrumental/vocal techniques used by Bach in this cantata.
4   Understand the form, textures and harmonies used in each movement.
5   Understand how Bach sets the text musically and what the text means.

Overview
- This cantata is a product of Bach's Leipzig period. It was written for the fourteenth Sunday after Trinity.
- It was at Leipzig, between 1723 and 1744, that Bach developed and perfected this form of the chorale cantata.
- The spirit of this form is that the entire chorale (hymn tune) becomes the basis of the cantata.
- The theme of this cantata is 'consolation'.
- It is one of the best-known Bach cantatas and was one of Felix Mendelssohn's favourite cantatas.

Tempo markings and terminology: there are very few actual tempo markings in the score. The tempo of the pieces would be worked out by the conductor/leader from the fastest note values in the piece that would be comfortably playable/singable for instrumentalists and singers.

Bass recitative:

- *vivace* – lively
- *adagio* – slowly
- *andante* – at a walking pace

Instrumental techniques and expression markings:

- *7# 65* etc. – (figured bass)
- *dal Segno* – return back to the sign
- *tr.* – trill
- *pizz.* – pizzicato (plucked)

Table 8.3

Bach Cantata BWV 78 Movement/Voices	Instruments
Chorus SATB	2 violins, viola, cello (as part of continuo), flute, 2 oboes, continuo (harpsichord), horn (doubling soprano line)
Aria Duet Soprano and Alto soloists	continuo (organ and cello) with double bass
Recitativo Tenor solo	continuo (organ or harpsichord and cello)
Aria Tenor solo	flute and continuo
Recitativo Bass solo	(accompanied recitative) 2 violins, viola and continuo
Aria Bass solo	oboe, 2 violins, viola and continuo
Chorale SATB Chorus	Tutti doubling the vocal lines: S — flute, oboe I, violin I, horn A — oboe II, violin II T — viola B — continuo

Analysis of Cantata BWV 78

Movement 1: Chorus

Form: ritornello

Key: g minor (but based on modulations in the Chorale: g minor – D – F – B flat – g minor).

Texture: Mainly polyphonic

- The Cantata BWV 78 opens with a magnificent chorale-fantasia; a profoundly expressive lament. Along with the chorale (hymn tune) sung in the soprano voice, its basic material is provided by a chromatically descending theme four bars in length (theme 1b).
- This recurring theme gives the movement the form of a chaconne or passacaglia. This is a set of continuous variations on the chromatic descending 'ground bass'. The descending chromatic theme expresses the great pain, anguish and suffering of Christ.
- This first movement starts with alternating orchestral (theme 1a) and canonic and melismatic choral passages, and reaches a climax in which the tutti orchestra and chorus play and sing in complex polyphony.
- In the 144 bars of the first movement there are 27 chaconne repetitions, two of which are in inversion, and several times it appears in the highest soprano part, or in other keys (subdominant or dominant).
- The chaconne repetitions occur in sequence 22 times. There are stretto-like entries before the cantus firmus (chorale – hymn tune, in the soprano part) appears.

Theme 1a

Theme 1b

Hymn theme

Movement 2: *Aria Duet*

Form: da capo aria (ternary) with the first instrumental introduction, and then vocal theme returning several times (ritornello-like).

Key: B flat major.

Texture: mainly polyphonic.

- The second movement, a duet for soprano and alto, is melodically one of the most enchanting movements written by Bach.
- Bach uses **word painting** in the opening line in the continuo instruments – 'We hasten with failing but diligent paces' – as suggested by the optimistic, bouncing, quaver theme (Theme 2a).
- The mood of this duet is a complete contrast to the slowly drooping figure of the first movement.
- Vocal characteristics include the **canonic** chasing of one voice after the other, the many antiphonal repeats of 'O Jesu' (Theme 2c) and 'zu dir' (Theme 2d), and the **coloraturas** on 'erfreulich'. The long, flowing, melismatic melodies of the A section contrast strongly with the short, punctuated words 'Ach! Hore, wie wir' in the B section. Imitation and sequential melodies are employed throughout.
- Bach personally marked the instrumental parts 'piano' whenever the voices enter. These unambiguous expression markings were an unusual feature of baroque composition.

Theme 2a

Theme 2b

The following two recitatives (Movements 3 and 5) paint a picture of the sinfulness of man.

Compared with these, the tenor and bass arias (Movements 4 and 6) are elegant and cheerful in mood: the tenor aria with its sustained joyful flute **obbligato**, and finally the serene bass aria with its optimistic **concertante** style.

Movement 3: *Tenor – Recitative Secco*

Form: structure comes from the text (syllabic setting apart from the final three bars).

Key: use of unresolved diminished chords keeps the listener on edge, as there is no tonal centre. The final bar ends in a perfect cadence on the note C.

Texture: homophonic.

- The mood is dramatised by the **large interval jumps** in the tenor voice and the great emphasis on the words of the text.
- There is a rare 'piano' dynamic marking in the continuo part. Such a marking only occurs in one other place in a Bach recitative (BWV 99).
- **Recitative secco** (secco means dry) – the vocalist and the continuo only.

Movement 4: *Tenor Aria*

Form: ritornello-like (flute and continuo introduction, interludes and coda) and ternary type form – A, B^1, B^2 voice.

Key: g minor.

Texture: homophonic – flute and continuo; polyphonic – flute, tenor and continuo.

- The flute's music is mainly linear with many ornate scale-like passages with some wide jumps that are nearly always the countermelody to the tenor's own intricate, melismatic setting, though the tenor and flute do play together in thirds in bars 51 and 52.

- The tenor also has many difficult wide intervals to pitch.
- There are many **sequences** within the flute music.
- There are elements of word-painting occurring in this g minor aria; a change to major on the words, 'macht mir das Herze wieder leicht'.

Movement 5: Bass – *Recitative Accompagnato*

Form: arioso-style recitative (more melodic than declamatory style).

Key: E flat major with modulations to g minor, A flat major and f minor.

Texture: mainly homophonic with a more contrapuntal texture in the Andante section (voice against strings and continuo).

- This recitative is rich in chromaticism.
- The secco (dry, continuo only) style changes to a sophisticated accompagnato (orchestrally accompanied) style as used in Bach's Passions.
- There are wide interval jumps to increase the dramatic and expressive power of the words, and also many sudden changes in tempo: *vivace – adagio – andante*. The indication *con ardore* (in the *vivace* section) increases the dramatic effect.
- Both syllabic and melismatic text setting.
- Notated ornamentation in vocal part.

Movement 6: *Bass Aria*

Form: da capo aria (ternary form – A, B, A^1) with ritornello-like oboe and string interludes (like a ripieno in a concerto).

Key: C minor.

Texture: homophonic – oboe, strings and continuo.

Polyphonic – bass against countermelody oboe with continuo and strings.

- This is more like a concerto for bass voice and oboe with the insertions of tutti passages for the strings.
- The strong main theme (below) is heard throughout the aria in both the oboe and violin 1 parts in c and g minors.

- Pedal notes, melismatic elaborate overlapping of parts between the voice and oboe and much use of ornamentation can be heard in this movement.
- Terraced dynamics (*forte* or *piano*) can be seen throughout this movement.

Movement 7: *Chorale*

Finally, the hymn tune proper (chorale) is heard in its unadorned setting (homophonic) by the SATB chorus and tutti orchestra.

Key: g minor but end in a tierce de picardie in G major.

Cadences every two bars: perfect (bar 2), imperfect (bar 4), perfect (bar 6), imperfect (bar 8), perfect into F major (bar 10), perfect into B flat major (bar 12), imperfect (in tonic bar 14) and finally, perfect into tonic major, G major (tierce de picardie) in final bar 16.

Tchaikovsky: *Romeo and Juliet* Fantasy Overture

Overview

- *Romeo and Juliet* Fantasy Overture is a concert overture written in sonata form: Introduction, Exposition, Development, Recapitulation and Coda.
- It is a piece of programme music. Tchaikovsky's objective was to create a general impression of Shakespeare's play.
- Tchaikovsky (1840–93) dedicated the *Romeo and Juliet* Fantasy Overture to Balakirev.
- It was first performed in Moscow in 1870, and was not successful. Tchaikovsky modified the work and the revised version was first performed in 1880.
- The overall form of the work is sonata form (or sonata allegro), with the Exposition being preceded by a long, slow Introduction. A final Coda closes the movement after the Development and Recapitulation section.

- Though there are only 522 bars in the overture, the time difference between recordings can be as much as 3 to 4 minutes. (Try and listen to a few different recordings and see which version you prefer: some can be very 'romantic' and texturally dense while others can be fast, light and nearly 'classical' in performance.)
- Use your full score to copy main themes and motifs (from all your set works) into your music manuscript. It may be tedious work but it really helps you to become better (neater, quicker and more meticulous) at music notation.

Tempo markings and terminology used in *Romeo and Juliet*:

- *andante non tanto quasi moderato* – literally 'at a walking pace, not too much, semi-moderately'
- *poco a poco string(endo) accel(erando)* – little by little getting faster and louder
- *allegro* – fast
- *molto meno mosso* – not as much
- *string(endo) al ...* – faster and louder to ...
- *allegro giusto* – fast and steady
- *moderato assai* – extremely moderate.

Listen to a recording of *Romeo and Juliet* and follow the chart of themes below:

Table 8.4   Themes in *Romeo and Juliet*

Romeo and Juliet	Friar Laurence	Subject I themes				Subject II themes	
	Chorale theme	SI Strife theme	String scales	Semitone 3-note idea	Canon	SIIa Love	SIIb
Introduction	✓						
Exposition		✓					
			✓				
				✓			
		✓					
				✓			
					✓		
				✓			
		✓					
			✓				
				✓			
		✓					

Romeo and Juliet	Friar Laurence	Subject I themes					Subject II themes	
	Chorale theme	SI Strife theme	String scales	Semitone	3-note idea	Canon	SIIa Love	SIIb
(Bridge)					✓			
							✓	
								✓
							✓ dev.	
							✓	
	✓ dev.							✓
Development		✓	✓					
	✓		✓					
				✓				
	✓	✓	✓					
		✓			✓			
Recap		✓						
			✓					
				✓				
		✓						
								✓
							✓ dev.	
							✓	
		✓						
	✓			✓				
		✓ dev.	✓					
Coda							✓ dev.	
	✓ dev.						✓	

Transposing instruments used:

- **Clarinet in A** sounds a minor third lower than written.
- **Cor anglais** sounds a perfect fifth lower than written.
- **Double bass** sounds an octave lower than written.
- **Horn in F** sounds a perfect fifth lower than written.
- **Piccolo** sounds an octave higher than written.
- **Trumpet in E** sounds a major third higher then written.

Table 8.5   Instruments used in *Romeo and Juliet*

P. I. Tchaikovsky (1840–93)	*Romeo and Juliet* Fantasy Overture	Instruments
		Full symphony orchestra used throughout. *Woodwind*: piccolo, 2 flutes, 2 oboes, 2 clarinets in A, cor anglais, 2 bassoons
		Brass: 4 horns in F, 2 trumpets in E, 2 trombones, bass trombone, tuba
		Percussion: 3 timpani, cymbals, bass drum
		Strings: violins I, violins II, violas, cellos and double basses and harp

Instrumental techniques and expression markings:

- *dolce* – sweetly
- *marc.* – marcato (accented)
- *a2* – two instruments play the same line of music
- *dolce ma sensibile* – sweetly but sensitively
- *espress.* – expressively
- *sempre* – always
- *pizz.* – pizzicato (plucked)
- *arco* – with the bow
- *div.* – divided
- *unis.* – unison
- *con sordini* – with mute
- *senza sordini* – without mute.

Analysis of *Romeo and Juliet* Fantasy Overture

Introduction

- The main theme used in the **Introduction** is the **Friar Laurence** theme, sometimes called the **Ecclesiastical** theme.
- Many other smaller melodic and rhythmic motifs occur in this very long and slow introduction. The theme is in two parts; a progression of woodwind chords that are supposed to represent Friar Laurence, and a following ascending and descending pattern in the strings and horns, later with winds.
- The theme is repeated down a semitone but two octaves higher in the flutes and oboes, in F minor, over pizzicato strings.

Key: F sharp minor (the tonic of the overall overture is b minor).

Metre: common time (4/4).

Texture: homophonic chorale.

Main instruments: two clarinets and two bassoons introduce the theme. All the instruments are involved at some point at the beginning of this introduction. Arpeggios on the harp are also a dominant feature.

Mood: tension and anticipation increasing and decreasing throughout by use of shifting block instrumentation, pedal notes, timpani rolls, chromatic variation of the theme and counterpoint and contrary motion in the string accompaniment.

Exposition

There are many different names for all the different themes and motifs in this work. Do *not* get confused by them. Once you are able to describe the theme and its musical characteristics that is all that is needed.

Within the exposition there are two distinct grouping of main themes; Subject I group and Subject II group. There is an obvious difference between the first and second subjects, as is the case in most sonata form movements. The first is rhythmic and strong, the second lyrical and legato.

Subject 1 (SI) – Strife theme

Key: SI is in B minor.

The first theme, in full orchestra, is supposed to represent the Montagu-Capulet feud. This theme can be further broken down into a further six motifs or sections, the first four being developed throughout the development and recap sections:

1   the opening bars of SI, the orchestral tutti
2   the ascending and descending semiquaver scale passages in the strings
3   the quaver semitone motif heard first in the wind and horns
4   the antiphonal and chromatic rising three-note motif
5   a version of SI by the lower strings followed by the high woodwind in canon (polyphonic)
6   running string semiquavers punctuated by loud brass, woodwind and percussion syncopated accents.

Texture: mainly homophonic.

Main instruments: tutti. Tchaikovsky's orchestration uses timbre (instrumental sound colour) in blocks of sound; sequences of strings against woodwind, etc.

Mood: formidable and powerful.

Features:

1 use of a chain of dominant sevenths

2 vibrant, full texture in B minor by the full orchestra

3 rushing scale passages in the strings (a common Tchaikovsky string orchestration)

4 an array of developed fragmented motifs, quaver, semiquaver and dotted rhythms and sequential scale passages are used by Tchaikovsky to hasten the music towards a *fortissimo* climax

5 what happens instead is a release of tension, a sudden *diminuendo*, and a transition (developing the rising three-note motif) leading to an unusual modulation to D flat (instead of to D major, the relative major of B minor) and the introduction of the SII melodies (Love theme).

6 the transitions are played above an A note (dominant) pedal and seem to be predicting the Love theme in D major. (We finally get the Love theme in D major in the Recap.)

Subject II (SII) – Love theme

There are two second subject themes: the Love theme proper, the universally renowned lyrical melody; and the shimmering muted string (diminished fifth) arpeggio figure.

Key: D flat major.

Texture: homophonic (first rendition), polyphonic (second rendition – with the descending 'sighing' countermelody motif on the horns).

Orchestration: cor anglais – muted violas (first time), flute and oboe (second time), flute, oboes and clarinets (third time). Strings used predominately as an accompaniment (used for melody in recap).

Features:

■ the eight-bar Love theme is accompanied by pizzicato cellos and double basses with French horns playing syncopated chords

■ sequential development of the Love theme is used

■ dominant pedal in the lower strings and bassoons help the harmonic suspensions and resolutions throughout this section

■ the flute and oboe ascending semiquaver scales leading to the recurrence of SII intensifies the passionate sentiment that Tchaikovsky is trying to achieve

■ rubato may be employed by the performers to give this theme a lush, romantic feel

■ the harp is again employed using descending alternating chord inversions

■ the lyrical mood peacefully dies away into silence. Tchaikovsky almost always ends his expositions this way, so that he can make a great contrast with the development

■ a viola F natural brings the exposition to a close.

Development

1   The development section is easily identifiable because the mood again becomes tense and violent.
2   Of the three main themes, the SII Love theme is not used in this development section.
3   The key signature of B minor has vanished and we are left sensing only a vague tonal centre.
4   SI motifs fragment into an urgent murmur in the strings, and the sequential patterns of the Friar Laurence theme is blazed out on the four horns. The brass and woodwind question each other in an antiphonal manner over syncopated string accompaniment.
5   The music reaches the first real fortissimo climax with a cymbal crash, and the Friar Laurence theme is then blasted by the two trumpets over a rhythmic ostinato taken from the opening of SI.
6   The key of B minor is finally established in the rushing semiquaver string scales that lead directly to the Recapitulation.

Recapitulation

Key: B minor

Themes: not all in the same order as before. Much development of these same themes occurs in this elongated section.

- You can tell you've reached the recapitulation because the SI theme is played in full, *tutti* (*ff*), for the first time since the beginning of the exposition.
- The second section of the Love theme enters first, and is played by winds instead of violins.
- The lyrical Love theme melody comes second, this time in the piccolo and strings, with triplet accompaniment in the wind along with the horn countermelody. It is to be played with all the feeling that the orchestra can summon.
- After the full statement the mood turns tense as the music goes into the minor mode.
- The Strife theme begins to re-emerge as the music leads into what is really a second development section within the recap.
- Tutti orchestra unites to increase the tension as the climax to the entire overture is reached.

Coda (the Funeral)

1   Triplet timpani ostinato rhythms open the quiet Coda section in B major.
2   The Love theme is played in the minor mode by bassoon, viola and cello, giving a sense of the final tragedy. It is followed by the full woodwind section playing Friar Laurence's chorale.

3 A final serene rendition of the Love theme is heard high in the strings before the
overture finishes with loud tutti syncopated tonic major chords over a timpani roll.

Queen: 'Bohemian Rhapsody'

By Freddie Mercury, from the Queen album *A Night at the Opera*, 21 November 1975.

- Freddie Mercury: piano and vocals
- Brian May: lead guitar
- Roger Taylor: percussion
- John Deacon: bass guitar.

The single was released on 31 October 1975 and was No. 1 for nine weeks in the UK. It
was championed by DJ Kenny Everett on Capital Radio, and Freddie Mercury won his
second Ivor Novello Award for the song, while the British Phonographic Industry awarded
it Best Single of 1975. The 'Bohemian Rhapsody' video was the first real 'music video'.

Why is/was 'Bohemian Rhapsody' such a big hit?

- good studio and video production
- catchy melody
- diversity in musical styles
- use of a non-standard song form
- non-regular phrasing
- limited use of repetition
- rhythm – use of off-beat accents, tricky syncopation, triplets and unusual
  metre(s)
- use of modulation
- use of unusual chord progressions
- harmonious melody and accompaniment
- overall cohesion without being predictable
- completely innovative in all respects
- skilful performance, especially live (operatic section pre-recorded for live
  gigs)
- good interplay between lyrics and music.

What you need to study about Queen and 'Bohemian Rhapsody':

1 style of Queen as a rock band
2 analysis: form, instrumentation, style and production of 'Bohemian Rhapsody'
3 recording techniques used in the making of the record
4 what influence 'Bohemian Rhapsody' has had since its release
5 the chordal progressions, keys and modulations used throughout.

Tempo markings and terminology used in 'Bohemian Rhapsody':

There is a mixture of English and Italian tempo markings:

- *l'istesso tempo* – the same speed (the beat remains the same when time signature changes)
- *poco a poco rit. e dim.* – little by little slowing and getting softer.

First and second time bars

The piano sheet music of 'Bohemian Rhapsody' does not have all the notated harmony lines, correct rhythmic notation, riffs and bridges in it. The basis for your study should be the recording.

Form

Introduction – Main Song – Operatic Section – Second Song – Recapitulation and Coda.

1   This six-minute song is a fusion of 1970s rock, pop and opera.
2   Many different compositional techniques are used, including: chromaticisms, diminished chords, imitative counterpoint, many changes of key and metre, abrupt modulations, unusual chordal inversions and sequences.
3   Throughout the work there are many motifs that are used in more than one section. This helps to link the many original stylistic sections.
4   'Bohemian Rhapsody' is particularly remarkable for several reasons, including the good interplay between lyrics and music (e.g. semantic meaning of chords).
5   Hardly any pop song reached the level of complexity of the more complex Queen songs.
6   The production was probably more complex than any previous hit record.
7   The song covered more styles, including a stylised opera-choir unprecedented on the singles market, maybe even in progressive rock circles.
8   At six minutes the song is relatively (but not uniquely) long.
9   The arrangement features the classic 'Queen combo': electric bass, drums, piano, double-tracked rhythm guitar, multi-track guitar choirs, multi-track vocal harmonies (sometimes up to six parts), and twelve tracks; nothing extra except the special percussion gong and the bell-tree.
10 Queen used to perform the song on stage without the Introduction, and the Opera section was played back from tape, providing a perfect spot for a light-show.
11 The basic harmonies of the first phrase: IGm7/DIC7 IF7 IB♭ I B♭
12 The first phrase features a chain of fifths. Note the heavy use of seventh chords here and throughout this first section.

13 The first verse is 15 and half bars long and is based on the progression: I B$^\flat$ 6 I Gm9 I Cm9 I Cm F I

14 The rhythm of the second song riff features triplets (hemiolas) in sympathy with the soon-to-enter lead vocal. Hemiolas dominate the lead vocal throughout the Rock section and create a strong feeling of a 6/4 meter (12/8), while the drums play a steady 4/4 backbeat. This is an example of simple polyrhythm.

Introduction

Key: B flat major.

Style: slow rock.

Metre: changing time signatures: 4/4 (5/4).

Melody: syncopated, repeated melody notes in chorus and solo voice, mainly stepwise motion, and harmony falling and rising by a semitone. Backing vocals overdubbed.

Instrumentation: vocals – a cappella (four-part close harmony vocals) and piano, then crash cymbal and bass guitar.

Texture: backing vocals, then piano accompaniment figure (piano broken chord motif).

Note:

- stereo panning (right to left, bar 11)
- flanged crash cymbal (synthesised) word painting of the wind blowing at bar 12
- chromatic descending bass line.

Features of the main song (two verses)

Key: B flat/E flat.

Style: ballad style.

Metre: 4/4 (2/4).

Texture: homophonic.

Melody: solo vocal, simple stepwise or triadic movement, octave range.

Instrumentation: solo voice, backing vocals, piano, bass and drum kit enters with cymbal crash and uses 'backbeat' (snaredrum accent on beats 2 and 4).

Accompaniment: developed piano broken chord accompaniment.

Note the following:

- bass guitar glissando
- descending chromatic scale in piano and bass guitar
- bass rhythm changes to minim

- syllabic word setting throughout
- word painting: the bell tree at 'shivers down my spine'.

Bridge after second verse

Key: E flat.

Style: heavy rock

Metre: 4/4.

Orchestration: lead guitar solo (lick) with bass and drums.

Note:

- chromatic descending bass line doubled on bass guitar and piano left hand. Dotted rhythm in bass
- sextuplet semiquavers descending passage followed by ascending syncopated scales in lead guitar. Makes use of bending notes, vibrato and glissando.

Operatic section

Key: A major, then A flat major.

Tempo: *l'istesso tempo* – new tempo's crotchet is the same as the old tempo's quaver, therefore it exactly doubles in speed.

Metre: 4/4 and 2/4.

Texture: homophonic and antiphonal singing (call and response).

Instrumentation: piano.

Melody: low chromatic melody with high pitched falsetto interjections (vocal solo, then chorus answer).

Note:

- use of diminished chords
- unexpected change of tempo, texture and key
- guitars and drums enter before the next section, the hard rock riff, building up into a rich texture
- rhythm section in triplets.

Second song

Key: E flat major.

Style: hard rock.

Metre: 12/8 (4/4).

Orchestration: lead guitar, bass guitar and drums, no piano.

Melody: solo voice in triplet rhythm, very high, extended range.

Texture: rich, homophonic.

Note:

- syncopated feel
- loudest section in song
- overdubbed guitar tracks with heavy, distorted guitar licks
- sudden D flat chord (flattened VII chord)
- lead guitar lick uses modulating scale patterns
- piano rejoins at bar 121 and the tempo slows.

Recap and Coda

Key: E flat, but ends on the chord of F major.

Style: slow rock.

Metre: 4/4.

Instrumentation: solo voice, overdubbed, panned guitars in imitation. Backing vocals ('ooh') recall the first song. Drums drop out. The gong and piano end the piece.

In this section:

- the tempo is freer (rubato)
- the texture is sparser.

Gerald Barry: Piano Quartet No. 1

Overview

This piece for piano, violin, viola and cello is in a contemporary, classical atonal idiom. Two Irish traditional melodies are used as the cornerstones of this distinct, sectional work.

Nua Nós, a contemporary Irish ensemble, premiered it on 6 December 1992.

Tempo markings and terminology used in Barry's Piano Quartet:

Only metronome markings are used for each section. Barry mixes 'mood' words and musical description of how to play the music with the metronome figure in a very detailed and exact manner eg: 'wild!', 'not slower!', 'with great verve and clarity', 'jauntily', 'subito!' (suddenly).

Example: ♩ = 126 Wild!

There are twenty different indications of metronomic time in this work.

> Score reading this work can be difficult because of the very fast tempos, changing pulses and contrapuntal textures. The work is very sectional and has distinct themes. Here are a few helpful pointers:
>
> - mark off each section in your score to enable you to identify the following section if you get lost
> - on your score write in 'slow', 'moderate', 'fast', etc. over the changing metronome marks
> - try to train your eye to score-read better by listening out for specific features or easily recognisable instrumental entries at certain points of the score
> - a blank score will not help your active listening.

Instrumental techniques and expression markings:

- *sim.* – play in a similar fashion
- *espressivo* – expressively
- *subito!* – suddenly
- *8ve* – play an octave higher (or lower, under the bass stave) than written
- *detaché* – detached
- *senza vibrato* – no vibrato
- *flautando* – bow near the fingerboard to produce 'flute-like' notes.

Play note on open string; pizzicato (plucked)

Harmonics

Features of Gerald Barry's compositional style

- Frequently changing time signatures give the work a vacillating pulse. The Piano Quartet has more than 330 changes of time signature in its 571 bars of music!
- Complex rhythmic patterns and rhythmic counterpoint are abundant in this work. Barry uses **polymetric rhythm** in this work: this means that different time signatures are superimposed on each other.

- Shape and line of melody and texture are more important compositional characteristics than timbre.
- Gerald Barry's music is very virtuosic. It is of extreme difficulty because the composer clearly indicates precise metronome marking for each section.
- Polyrhythm, changing pulses in rapidly changing time signatures and atonal melodies that performers find difficult to learn off by heart do not bode well for the performer of Barry's music.
- Canon is the most common compositional device that Barry uses. This contrapuntal technique is used in the majority of sections. The range and distance of the canon vary in each section.
- Other compositional techniques that Barry utilises are: retrograde; inversion; and transposition.

Form of Barry's Piano Quartet No. 1

A B^1 C^1 C^2 B^2 C^3 D^1 D^2+B^3 E C^4 C^5 E^2+D^3 C^6 C^7 F+C^8 C^9 G H

Analysis

Table 8.6   Analysis of Barry's Piano Quartet No. 1

Section		Features	
A	Si Bheag, Si Mhór (C major!) Two parts	Four- and five-part canon at ♩ Inversion of Irish tune	Tutti Extremes in register in second part Heard once only
B^1	'Village Band' Dissonances Changing metre	Three variations of this tune Open fifth accompaniment	Vln & Vla + Cello + Hand clusters on piano
C^1	A flat tonality Senza vibrato Calm section, then suddenly violent	Irregular, jerky rhythms Contrapuntal texture	Vln, Vla, VC + Pno
C^2	'Spirit of viol' playing in sixteenth-century style — two parts	Bigger melodic intervals than C1	Vla & VC + Vln

Section		Features	
B²	B melody played five times	Three-part canon Contrasting texture and mood	Vln, Vla, VC + Pno (RH then LH)
C³	C melody played four times. Viol playing – atonal	Violin and cello homophonic and very dissonant	Vln, Vla, VC + Pno (fragments) violin descant superimposed
D¹	New material – A minor	Rhythmically volatile – jazzy	Vla & VC only
D²+B³	D2 on violin and piano	B3 on viola, cello and piano (left hand)	Rhythmically distorted
E	E1 is the retrograde of D2	Four-part canon at ♪	Piano (LH) & Vln, Vla, VC
C⁴	Hommage á Horowitz	Piano octaves of C2	Solo piano
C⁵	Violin part of C3 played twice	Three-part canon	Vln, Vla, VC
E²+D³	E2 is retrograde of D with D also	Transposed into B flat minor	D3 – VC and Pno E2 – Vln and Vla
C⁶	Shorter version of C5	Transposed Flautando	Vln, Vla, VC
C⁷	Sounds new but is inverted C music	Striding	Tutti
F+C⁸	Augmented C2 in Vla and VC	Polymetry: 2/2 v 3/4 etc.	F in the Vln – retrograde in the Pno
C⁹	Slowest C section music	Two octaves between parts	Vln, Vla, VC
G	Fragments telescoped together	First and last moments of each section	Tutti
H	Lord Mayo's Delight	Two- and three-part canons Heard once only	Vla & VC + Pno + Vln

Set Works: Group B

(To be examined in 2008–10.)

- W. A. Mozart, Piano Concerto No. 23 in A, K488 (1798)
- Hector Berlioz, Symphonie Fantastique (1830)
- The Beatles, *Sgt Pepper's Lonely Hearts Club Band* (1967)
- Raymond Deane, *Seachanges (with Danse Macabre)* (1993)

Quick Revision – Set Works B

Table 8.7

Work	Movement/ Section	Time Signature	Key Signature	Style	Tempo
Mozart (1756–91) Piano Concerto No. 23, K. 488	I	C	A major	Classical solo concerto	Allegro
	II	6/8	F# minor		Adagio
	III	¢	A major		Allegro assai
Berlioz (1803–69), Symphony Fantastic	II Un Bal (The Ball); waltz	3/8	A major	Romantic symphonic programme music	Allegro non troppo
	IV Marche au Supplice (March to the Scaffold)	¢	G minor (ends in G major)		Allegretto non troppo
The Beatles, *Sergeant Pepper's Lonely Hearts Club Band*	'Sergeant Pepper's Lonely Hearts Club Band'	4/4	G major	Popular songs with instrumental accompaniment	Moderately slow, with a strong beat
	'She's Leaving Home'	3/4	E♭ major		Moderate
	'When I'm Sixty-four'	¢	C major		Steady 2 beat

Work	Movement/ Section	Time Signature	Key Signature	Style	Tempo
Deane (b. 1953), *Seachanges with Danse Macabre*	I	Many time signatures	No tonal key signature. Atonal, but based on three-note cell: G, A, C	Contemporary quintet for mixed ensemble	♩ = 80
	II	7/4			♩ = 120
	III	6/4 3/2			♩ = 80
	IV	7/8 7/4			♩ = 120
	V	6/4 3/2			♩ = 80
	VI	7/4			♩ = 120

Revision of Instruments – Set Works B

Table 8.8   **Instruments used in Set Works B**

Composer	Vocal	Strings	Woodwind	Brass	Percussion	Keyboard/ Other
Mozart		✗	✗	✗		✗
Berlioz		✗	✗	✗	✗	
Beatles	✗	✗	✗	✗	✗	✗
Deane		✗	✗		✗	✗

Listening Paper I – Recognition of instruments is always tested in the exam. Knowing what instruments are used in each set work and in each section of each set work is a great foundation for Paper I.

In the months preceding your exam, you should listen to all your set works *at least* ten times in your own study or revision time. It is the only way fully to understand each set work.

CD recordings of most Leaving Certificate Set Works are available from your local music shop, or ask your teacher.

Mozart: Piano Concerto No. 23 in A Major K488

Overview

- The A major concerto K488 was one of three piano concertos written during the winter of 1785–86, while Mozart was also at work on his opera *The Marriage of Figaro*.
- Mozart himself probably premiered it during March 1786.
- The concerto uses clarinets in place of oboes, and Mozart's emphasis on the woodwinds can be felt early in the movement. The pianist's role is a little subdued in the first movement, but there are some brilliant flashes in the cadenza.
- This concerto is set in the usual three-movement form. It is one of his most attractive works, contrasting a refined opening movement with a pathos-laden second movement and a bubbling, cheerful finale.
- The dialogue of the piano and orchestra cannot be reduced to a simple alternation of 'tutti' and 'solo' sections; the soloist engages in a constant exchange of ideas with smaller or larger groups from the ensemble.
- The concerto combines in its music a symphonic expression with the soloist's brilliance and wealth of ideas, all of which is set against the backdrop of a supremely clear-cut form.
- The key of F sharp minor (a romantic key), the tonic of the slow second movement, is extremely rare in Mozart's output – in fact, this is the only time it is used as the main key of any entire movement in all of Mozart's works.

Instrumental techniques and expression markings

- ∾ – mordant (turn)
- *pizz.* – plucked
- *arco* – with the bow
- *tutti* – all instruments playing
- *zu 2* – same as *a2*, two instruments play in unison
- *cadenza* – a virtuosic, improvised section by the soloist
- *tr.* – trill.

The opening movement is in the classical sonata form, involving a double exposition. The Adagio, lyrical and extremely tender, is in three parts with the return of the opening section, and the finale follows a Rondo pattern.

At the outset, the slow movement is unusual in two ways. It is Mozart's first piano concerto slow movement to be labelled *Adagio*. (*Andante* or *Larghetto* are more common.) Also, Mozart wrote it in the key of F sharp minor, a 'romantic' key rarely found in his music.

Analysis

Key: A major.

Form: sonata form.

Number of bars: 313 (excluding cadenza).

The first movement is set in a modified sonata form, as was typical of Classical concertos. Mozart uses a double exposition.

The **trill** over a dominant seventh chord was the device used in classical concerto cadenzas for the soloist to signal to the orchestra their return.

This cadenza tells us a great deal about Mozart the improviser: besides virtuosic passages, it also contains expressive, singing music, and expands on the concerto's thematic material in simple yet ingenious ways.

Mozart refrains from always repeating material exactly, and keeps a feeling of freshness through allowing the pianist to embellish the main themes.

Active Listening – themes

First movement

Table 8.9   Themes in Mozart's Piano Concerto K488

Exposition	Piano Exposition	Codetta	Development	Recapitulation	Coda
SIa	SIa	Theme E	Use of	SIa	SIIb
SIb*	SIb		Theme E	SIb	
SIIa	SIIa			SIIa	
SIIb	SIIb			SIIb	
	SIb			Theme E	
				Cadenza	
Key: A	A—E	E	E, em, C, am, F, E–A	A	A

* SIb is *never* heard played in the piano part

Exposition

In Classical concerto sonata form there is typically a **double exposition**. This means that the main first and second subjects are presented by the orchestra alone, and then by the soloist. The orchestra's exposition presents both subjects in the tonic key.

The soloist begins their exposition in the tonic key with the first subject, but modulates for the second subject.

SI – first subject

- The strings open the work in the tonic key of A major. After eight bars the wind take up the same theme and close it in the tonic with a repeated perfect cadence.
- The section ends with loud, alternating tonic and dominant chords over a dominant pedal (E). Dotted rhythms in the wind leave the music hanging in mid-air, preparing the way for the second subject.

SII – second subject

- The second subject, played by Violins I, is a very graceful theme characterised by its gentle, occasionally chromatic, falling lines.
- The theme consists of two bars, which are used in a descending sequence and then developed. The repeated notes accentuate the bass line that descends stepwise for the first four bars. The theme is restated with the flute and bassoon joining in.

Piano entry

- The piano enters with a simple statement of SI with left-hand Alberti bass accompaniment. Melodic decoration, arpeggiated figures and fast scalic figures then decorate the original melodic themes in the part of the exposition.
- The modulation to the dominant, E major, finally happens when flute, bassoon and violin I play SII, with the piano enhancing the texture by doubling it in broken octaves.
- Strings imitate the wind an octave higher while the piano drives the music forward with sparkling semiquaver runs.
- Long trills are often used to emphasise important cadential points.
- The original material is now heard transposed into the dominant key.
- A new theme (Theme E) appears at bar 143. This gentle theme is used throughout the development section.

Development

- This new 'development' material is developed and the sense of tonality is destabilised.
- Mozart makes great use of textural contrast here by juxtaposing legato winds with staccato strings in segments of two bars each.
- Mozart uses sequential and imitative development through numerous keys, the harmony following the 'cycle of fifths'.

- This involves both orchestra and soloist, and culminates in a dominant pedal, bring the tonality back to the original tonic.
- The piano uses arpeggiated and scalic figures to elaborate on the sustained harmonies in the orchestra.

Recapitulation

- The recapitulation begins with the orchestra recalling the first subject in the tonic key of A major, reproducing the orchestral version of the first subject from bars 1–8.
- Originally just played by the strings, this time the wind join in and double some of the parts.
- The pianist then enters with an embellished second half of the theme: added grace notes, falling arpeggiations and scales a tenth apart.
- The recapitulation continues to be based on the soloist's version of the exposition.
- The use of the dominant pedal of E is prevalent.
- The soloist recalls the second subject, transposed up a perfect 4th into the tonic key of A major.
- The orchestra take over the theme as they did in the exposition.
- The soloist again decorates this with broken RH octaves.
- The piano alone plays a lengthy passage of virtuoso writing while the orchestra develops themes in an imitative manner similar to that in the development section.
- The bass line slides chromatically from here to land on a tonic chord in second inversion, full of expectancy for the soloist to leap into a virtuosic **cadenza.**
- A paused tonic chord in second inversion in the orchestra prompts the soloist to perform a cadenza.
- Movement ends with perfect cadences in the tonic.

Adagio, second movement

- The second movement's dominating sentiment in many ways foreshadows musical Romanticism.
- It begins with a gentle melody, played *piano*, expressed by the many naturals instead of sharps.
- The melody moves in the quiet rhythm of a *siciliano*: an Italian dance in compound metre with a swaying rhythm and a pastoral theme.
- It contains many expressive wide leaps, emphasising chromatic semitone movement and the melancholy-sounding 'Neapolitan sixth' chord.

Form: ternary – A (A1, A2, A3) B A (A1, A2, A2 Coda).

Key: F sharp minor.

Metre: 6/8.

A

The piano introduces the main theme of this movement. Dotted rhythms, large interval jumps and irregular phrasing combined with the f#m key and slow tempo produce a theme full of melancholy and pathos.

The instrumental second theme answers the opening piano statement. The sequential use of imitative canon at a third between the clarinet, bassoon and first violins is sublime. The chugging arpeggic accompaniment keeps the melodic line in a strict tempo so that the suspensions/resolutions of the melody will not be lost by over-zealous players.

The third theme, heard on piano for the two full statements, is an ornamented, chromatic descending scale which is then developed and a modulation to the relative major, A major, occurs.

B

This spirited middle section utilises the full stylistic and technical flexibilities of the clarinet. Left-hand arpeggios in the piano are contrasted with right-hand demi-semiquaver runs.

A

Mozart develops the main themes but keeps the orchestration quite similar to the opening section. New textures are added in the **Coda**, the sighing melody from the canon is heard against a repeated piano dominant notes before the movement gradually fades away.

Allegro assai, third movement

Table 8.10   Third movement: themes

Exposition	Development Section	Recapitulation	Coda
SIa Theme A	Episodes	Theme B	SIa 'A' SIIb
SIb	Theme E	SIIa 'C'	'D' Finale
Theme B	Theme F	SIIb 'D'	based on SIb
SIIa Theme C			
SIIb Theme D			
SIa (codetta or transition)			
Key: A–em–E	F#m—D—A	A—am—A	A—D—A

SIa is Theme A, the recurring main theme of the rondo. It is also the First subject (SI) 'a' theme – SIa.

SIb is a motif in the first subject group. It is not a recurring theme in the rondo but is used at the very end of the concerto.

Theme B could also be called SIc, as it is part of the first subject grouping. In sonata form proper, it would be a bridge theme before the second subject melodies.

Form: an extended **sonata-rondo**: a recurrent first theme alternates with a number of episodes (rondo), but unusually one of those episodes also returns, as a second theme would do in a sonata recapitulation. The fusion of these two forms results in a structure that allows the main melodies to be heard over and over again, while the alternations and developments of those melodies afford Mozart infinite diversity in compositional development.

Metre: cut common time.

Key: A major.

Mozart offers an overabundance of themes with some drama in the middle before the high spirits of the opening return to carry the concerto to its finish.

Exposition

Solo piano introduces this fast and virtuosic movement. The main theme, A, consisting of large interval jumps followed by a descending scale pattern accompanied by Alberti bass in the left hand. The orchestra then takes up the theme.

Mozart uses alternating blocks of opposing timbre in theme Ib, strings against woodwind. The woodwind timbres of the first movement return.

Theme B is also introduced by solo piano. The harmonic and melodic pace seem to slow with this graceful melody. In the bars following each statement of the main themes Mozart develops the musical motifs and gives an opportunity for the technical fluency of the soloist to shine.

The second subject group (Theme C) is introduced by flute and bassoon. The music continues with the piano's never-ending run of arpeggios and scales and with varying styles of accompaniment. Theme D is introduced again in the piano over pizzicato chords in the strings.

Development

Two new contrasting episodes are introduced in this section: an f# minor scale passage (Theme E); and a structured D major lyrical melody. Mozart's development of the musical material is perfect. The fragments of themes are always audible, the texture, while interesting, is not over-complicated, while the modulations are flawless.

Recapitulation

An ornamented version of Theme B is established by the soloist and repeated by the woodwind. Theme C, the minor-sounding theme, now has a tonality change to A major.

The music strides forward with richer textures and more counterpoint before the **coda** is introduced. These tutti passages are as bright and lively as Mozart had ever composed.

Table 8.11   Instruments used in Mozart's Piano Concerto K488

Strings	Woodwind	Brass	Keyboard
Violins I and II	1 Flute	2 Horns in A	Piano
Violas	2 Clarinets in A (sounds a third lower than written)	(sounds a third lower than written).	(wooden framed piano).
Cellos	2 Bassoons	These horns had no valves so could only play the harmonic series. Used mainly for filling out texture.	The range of dynamics would not be as great as today's instruments
Double Basses (double the cello line at an octave below)	No oboes were used by Mozart in this orchestration: he favoured the clarinet's timbre and flexibility.		

Hector Berlioz: Symphony Fantastique, Op. 14

'Episode in the life of an artist.'

Overview

- Berlioz's only symphony, Symphony Fantastique has become an icon of the Romantic era.
- Though in an early romantic genre, Berlioz's music was stylistically original.
- The symphony follows a five-movement structure (like Beethoven's Sixth Symphony, the 'Pastoral').
- Just like Beethoven, Berlioz provides the movements with headings and lays out a story that the symphony will follow.
- But, going even further than Beethoven in instrumentation, atmosphere and structure, Berlioz laid out the concept of what is now called **programme music.**
- The five movements express Berlioz's dreams regarding his obsession with Harriet Smithson (an Irish actress).

- Berlioz distributed the programme notes to the audience before the performance of the symphony. This provides some musical understanding to the listener.
- Berlioz is surprisingly modern; he uses a very large orchestra.
- Colourful orchestration is used throughout, including bells, cor anglais, two harps, multi-divisi strings, timpani and a large brass section.
- Berlioz's loved one is represented by an **idée fixe** (a principle later adopted by Wagner – the **leitmotif**). All of the movements are unified by a recurring theme, the idée fixe. The idée fixe is musically varied in each movement.
- Berlioz broke with tradition, the second movement (Valse: Un Bal) taking the place of the traditional scherzo.

Tempo markings and terminology

Berlioz uses a mixture of Italian and French tempo markings:

- *Valse. Allegro non troppo* – not too fast, waltz speed
- ♩ = 60 – metronome mark, 60 crotchets per minute (one per second)
- *rall ... a tempo* – slowing ... back to speed
- *sans retenir* – without holding back
- *I° tempo* – original tempo
- *animez* – animated (faster)
- *un peu retenu* – a little held back
- *rall. poco* – a little slower
- *I° tempo con fuoco* – original tempo with fire
- *serrez* – densely
- *Allegretto non troppo* – not too fast.

Instrumental techniques and expression markings

- *pizz.* – plucking
- *arco* – with the bow
- *div. (diviso)* – divided (instrumental parts)
- *unis.* – unison
- *baguettes d'éponge* – use soft sticks (timpani)
- *faites les sons bouchés avec le main sans employer les cylinders* – put hand in the bell (horns)
- *avec les cylinders, tous les son ouvert* – open bell (horns)
- *a 4 soli* – (all 4 bassoons play one line)
- *étouffez le son avec la main* – dampen the sound with your hand
- *soli* – plural of solo
- *sempre* – always
- *mf* – editorial dynamic marking

- ■ *8* – play one octave higher than written
- ■ *dolce e tenero* – sweetly and held
- ■ *poco* – little
- ■ *presque rien* – almost nothing
- ■ *espressivo* – expressively
- ■ *canto* – singing
- ■ *molto* – much
- ■ *flauto 2 muta in flauto piccolo* – second flute to piccolo
- ■ *rinf* – rinforzando (play very loud and come away suddenly)
- ■ *observez bien ici, la difference entre le fort et le demi-fort* – be careful of the difference between ff and mf
- ■ *dim. (diminuendo)* – dying away.

Instruments used in Symphony Fantastique

- ■ two flutes, two oboes, two clarinets in A, four bassoons
- ■ four horns, two trumpets, two cornets, three trombones, two ophicleides (a tuba-like instrument)
- ■ four timpani, cymbals, bass drum, side drum
- ■ strings (violins I, violins II, violas, cellos and double basses) and two harps.

Second movement, *Un Bal*

This movement begins with a sense of anticipation.

Form: ternary – Introduction A B A Coda.

Key: A major.

Metre: 3/8.

Introduction

Tremolo strings and ascending arpeggios in major, minor and diminished chords set the mood of anticipation. Descending scales form a perfect cadence in the tonic. This leads to an oom-pah-pah waltz-type accompaniment in the strings.

A Main theme 1

The waltz theme. A lyrical sixteen-bar melody in Violin I uses rubato to heighten the romantic feeling.

Simple tonic arpeggios on harp and lower strings introduce Theme 2, again in Violin 1. This theme is a descending scale. The answering phrase (both of five bars in length) uses semiquaver triplets in a ornamental 'turn' like fashion and employs chromatics.

Flute and clarinets provide the bridge, a major scale in thirds, to Theme 3. The opening phrase to this melody is a descending sequence of repeated notes while the texture of the answering phrase is polyphonic. A canon is used in contrary motion (Violin 1 and cello).

Theme 1 is repeated with a varied accompaniment of strings, harp and wind chords on each quaver beat respectively.

B *The idée fixe* is interwoven into this middle episode in the distant key of F major, despite the ongoing waltz rhythm, appearing in the flute and oboe (then flute and clarinet).

The accompaniment is extremely soft tremolo violin and viola murmurs above staccato arpeggios in cello and bass.

The accompaniment becomes more substantial and contrapuntal as the violins overlap with a semiquaver descant.

A *the recapitulation* uses the three main themes again in the tonic, A major, with an elongated and developed Theme 1 being repeated. The orchestration is much fuller and the texture more polyphonic in Theme 1 and 3 with ornamented Violin 1 lines and more use of block harmony in the wind in Theme 2.

The idée fixe appears in the coda; a solo clarinet over a horn pedal note. A much faster tutti rendition of SI leads to the cadential ending.

Fourth Movement, *Marche au Supplice*

Berlioz's earlier abandoned opera *Les Francs Juges* was the inspiration for this dark fourth movement, *Marche au Supplice* (March to the Scaffold), where he dreams that he has murdered his beloved and been condemned to die 'at the scaffold'.

Key: g minor (March section in B flat major – piece ends in G major).

Metre: cut common time.

Form: Introduction, Main Section 1 (descending theme), Main Section 2 (March theme), Transition, Development, Coda.

It starts with a great crescendo, the opening timpani ostinato and syncopated bassoon and horn figure successfully creating the tension.

The main melodies, the descending theme's eclectic instrumentation and the dotted march theme, are expertly orchestrated by the full orchestral forces.

The descending theme (two octaves) is a scale of g melodic minor. It is first heard in the cellos and basses and ends in an imperfect cadence. The second rendition of this theme adds violas with the four bassoons playing a syncopated countermelody. The third time the violins play the descending theme in E flat two octaves higher in pitch. A walking bass accompaniment is heard in the lower strings. The fifth rendition uses the descending theme in inversion and contrary motion in the strings accompanied by the bassoon playing a staccato walking bass.

Timpani B flats and the sweep of a B flat scale on strings introduce the March theme. A syncopated, dotted fanfare is played by wind and brass. This theme is repeated.

Berlioz uses antiphonal blocks of sound, brass answered by woodwind, and fragments the descending theme until the March theme is reiterated in B flat again, this time with elaborate string accompaniments.

A thick textured section follows, the trombones and bassoons blaring out a sequential development of the descending theme against a sextuplet accompaniment in woodwind and rising ornamented crotches in the strings.

An *ff tutti* statement of the descending theme is heard in the tonic. Dotted string fragments are juxtaposed against wind repeated chords and the tension increases.

Suddenly, the sparsely contrasted idée fixe appears in the clarinet just before the execution by guillotine, the loud cadential conclusion ending in G major (tierce de picardie).

The Beatles: *Sgt Pepper's Lonely Hearts Club Band*

Band members:

- Paul McCartney – vocals and bass guitar
- John Lennon – vocals and guitar
- George Harrison – lead guitar and vocals
- Ringo Starr – drums.

Producer and arranger: George Martin

The album was No. 1 for 27 weeks in the UK and No. 1 for 19 weeks in the US.

When listening to this recording try to be conscious of the:
1   unusual chord progressions
2   static melody
3   counterpoint in the horn interlude
4   drum kit/guitar backbeat patterns
5   John Lennon's distinctive voice in the chorus
6   descending chromatic bass guitar line

       & DS al Coda – Dal Segno al Coda – back to the sign and then to the Coda

       – pause

tacet – silence.

'Sgt. Pepper's Lonely Hearts Club Band'

Key: G Major

Metre: 4/4

Tempo: Moderately slow, with strong beat

Form: Intro (instrumental) I Verse I Bridge (instrumental) I Refrain (Chorus) I Bridge (vocal) I Verse I Coda (segue or link)

Album: *Sgt. Pepper's Lonely Hearts Club Band*, UK release: 1 June 1967; US release: 2 June 1967

Recorded: 1 and 2 February, 3 and 6 March 1967, Abbey Road

Additional Instruments: four French horns (players from the London Philharmonic Orchestra).

Mood: the mood is one of vibrancy. The loud rock sounds and recording studio effects of audience and orchestra tuning up give an impression of an open-air concert.

Style and form: 'Beatlesque' style. Hard syncopation and bluesy bent notes, but it still sounds very 1960s rock/pop-like.

Only two minutes in length (and remember, about ten seconds of that two minutes is the opening mix of crowd and tuning noise!).

Melody and harmony. Use of the crowd noise: in the opening seconds of the track you hear a rather passive audience chatting non-descriptively amongst themselves, backed by the string section tuning. But once the proceedings get under way, the audience gets participative, and applause and laughter are featured. The final verse provides more applause, building into screaming – maybe Beatlemania!

The vocal arrangement – Paul McCartney's rocky solo in the verses with a chorus being provided by the other band members, for the refrain and second bridge.

Introduction

The track fades in with more than ten seconds of concert hall audience ambience and orchestral tuning.

Lead guitar takes over the melody in a quasi bluesy-rock style.

The opening chord is not chord I. It is V^7 of V, a very typical Beatles chord (the dominant of the dominant – secondary dominant). This unconventional harmony at the start of a piece is also used in 'A Hard Day's Night' and 'Help!'.

Verse

The verse is a standard eight bars long. The melodic shape is quite static, which gives a rhetorical, declamatory feel to the singing.

The vocal part of the last four bars of the verse places repeated emphasis on the flattened blues third, turning the C chord into a C7, and creating a major-minor **cross-relation** in the last against the tonic chords.

Bridge

The instrumental bridge is five bars long; much **reverb** used. It is played in a contrapuntal style by the four French horns. The two bridges are differentiated by their different arrangements and melodic content.

The instrumental bridge opens with a V^7 (dominant seventh) chord on C, and this makes the first half of the music sound like a modulation to the key of F major (a distance key from the tonic, G major).

Refrain

This is the song's main chorus and it is the longest of the sections. It reiterates many times the words of the title. Harmonic dissonances are abundant:

- the major/minor switch on the I chord (with the minor one presented in first inversion)
- the appoggiatura on the C chord
- the bluesy minor third in the tune clashing with the D chord and the implied V^9 chord.

Coda

Chords vamped over a stepwise descending bass line: direct segue into the next track, an interesting experiment on this album.

'She's Leaving Home'

When listening to this recording try to be conscious of the:

- word painting
- syncopated rhythms in strings
- counterpoint in instruments and voices in refrain
- unusual phrasing
- melodic line in cellos.

Listen carefully to see if you can hear the viola and double bass.

Key: E major in the stereo recording (F major in the mono recording) and E flat major in the piano score.

Metre: 3/4.

Tempo: moderately.

Form: Intro I Verse 1 I Refrain I Verse 2 I Refrain I Verse 3 I Refrain I Coda

Recorded: 17 and 20 March 1967, Abbey Road 2.

Instrumentation: a string nonet (four violins, two violas, two cellos and double bass) and harp. It is the first song on the album not to include guitars and drums.

Mood: melancholy

Melody and harmony:

- an intentionally over-lush impression is created with the wide sweeping range of the melody
- teeming usage of seventh and ninth chords
- use of flattened seventh notes and minor v (dominant) – Mixolydian modal feeling
- the backing vocals for the refrains feature an unusual kind of antiphonal counterpoint
- the string parts fill the spaces between verse phrases and anticipate some of the melodic play of the refrain
- no modulations in this piece.

Introduction

The introduction consists of four bars of harp playing an elaborate arpeggio in the tonic chord.

Verse

The homophonic verse is in the phrase pattern ABB. The harmonic rhythm continually slows down.

There is a rising and falling melodic minor countermelody in the cellos.

Syncopated rhythms and contrary motion patterns in the strings break the constant simple 3/4 accompaniments.

The third verse is much shorter, having an AB pattern.

Refrain *(Chorus)*

Polyphonic – counterpoint in the two vocal parts (nearly antiphonal singing). Both voices are **double tracked** to produce a **chorus effect**.

Unusual length phrases – interrupted by three accented II^9 chords.

Harmonically, V-of-V (secondary dominant) is allowed to resolve directly to I (tonic) at the start of the next verse, without the benefit of the V (dominant) chord intervening.

Coda

The final refrain includes the echoing of the harp arpeggio of the introduction.
The V-of-V to IV is a much favoured progression of the Beatles, though the plagal IV–I final cadence echoes the faintly religious sentimentality.

'When I'm Sixty-Four'
Key: C major (piano score), D flat major (original recording).

Metre: 4/4.

Tempo: steady 2 beat.

Form: Intro | Verse | Bridge | Verse | Bridge | Verse | Coda

Recorded: 6, 8, 20 and 21 December 1966, Abbey Road 2.

Features: stylised nostalgic/vaudeville (music hall) song.

In the context of *Sgt Pepper*'s running order, it provides a well-needed contrast to the preceding track.

The song is mastered in the key of D flat, though it was recorded in the key of C in order to sound higher on playback and give Paul McCartney's lead vocal a younger, more earnest quality.

There is no doubling up of any sections, and the intro and coda use the same material.

There is no specific refrain section, though the verse here is of the type whose last phrase is refrain-like.

Melody and Harmony: the tune is built primarily out of triadic riffs and chromatic runs. The harmony is very straightforward, yet because of the chromaticisms of the melody, there are many added note chords: e.g. V^{13}, and harmonising of the chromatic bass line motion.

Additional Instruments:

Piano, two clarinets and a bass clarinet, tubular bell chimes.

Vocals: Paul McCartney (main singer); John Lennon and George Harrison (backing vocals).

Introduction

The band is vamping in true vaudeville style. Dotted rhythm with heavy accents in **cut common metre.**

Verse

Chromatically rising bass lines of the second and fourth phrases. Each of the phrases commences with the same chord with which the previous phrase ended.

Phrases plan: ABA'C.

Bridge

The bridge is an unusual seventeen bars long; sixteen plus one. The harmony in this section suggests a modal modulation to the key of the relative minor, and then back to the tonic key.

The arrangement of the two bridges: the first one starts off with one whole phrase minus vocalist-instrument interlude. But then the vocalist comes in for the second phrase, yet he drops out again for the downbeat of the third phrase. Then, the second time around, the singer sings in the first phrase, but still drops out at the beginning of the third phrase.

Raymond Deane: *Seachanges (with Danse Macabre)*

Understand and be familiar with:

- the sections, form and structure of the piece
- all compositional devices used: harmonic, melodic, rhythmic and metric
- the instruments used in each section
- the workings of the tone row (main melody)
- the modern instrumental techniques used by each instrument
- the themes and sentiment behind the work.

Themes and Inspiration
- A chamber work dealing irreverently with the theme of 'death'.
- The grey, misty Irish Atlantic versus the clear, bright Mexican Pacific.
- Mexican iconography, which is morbid, grotesque and gaudily melodramatic.
- Shakespeare's 'Full Fathom Five my Father Lies' – song from *The Tempest*.
- The American composer, Conlon Nancarrow, was a resident of Mexico. The canon between violin and marimba is dedicated to him.

Instruments used in *Seachanges*
- Piccolo and alto flute.
- Piano.
- Crotales (bells), maracas, gong, bass drum, tambourine, marimba, guiro (washing block), rain stick, cymbals.
- Violin and cello.

The Mexican or exotic instruments (the guiro, maracas, guitar (strumming like a guitar on the cello and violin) and marimba) contrast sharply with the European instruments: the piccolo and alto flute (high pitched timbres may represent the sounds of seabirds) and the piano (used melodically to represent the misty Irish coastline on a dull morning).

No Italian tempo marking are used in *Seachanges* and there are only two strict metronome markings which alternate throughout the piece:

 = 80 and ♩ = 120

Instrumental Techniques in *Seachanges*
- *15ma* – play 2 octaves higher than written – harmonics
- *con ped.* – with pedal
- – tremolo

- *pizz +* – left-hand pizzicato
- *8va* – play one octave higher than written
- *l.v.* – let vibrate
- *arco* – play with the bow
- *col legno bat.* – play with the wood of the bow
- *sec. (secco)* – dry (no pedal)
- *gliss.* – glissando (slide)
- *fz.* – (flute, flutter tonguing)
- *tr.* – trill
- *U.C.* – una corda (left 'soft' pedal on piano)
- *sul pont.* – play near the bridge
- *strum* – strum cello like a guitar
- *8_ba* – play an octave lower than written
- *sul tasto* – bow over the fingerboard
- *modo ord.* – play normally
- *molto vib.* – much vibrato
- *loco* – place, cancelling an 8_ba marking etc.
- *sempre* – always
- *sfffz* – sforzandissimo, (suddenly very, very loud)
- *non troppo cresc.* – not too much louder.

Contrasts in Dynamics and Timbres
- An important feature of this work is the huge dynamic range and varied and sudden dynamic contrasts.
- The use of resonant instruments (cymbals, crotales, gong) are also well contrasted against the *sec.* (dry) sounds; *pizz+*, maracas and syncopated piano chords.

- The piano acts as a link between the dynamic and resonant timbre qualities of all the other instruments.

Analytical Features

The **main motif** of *Seachanges* is the '**three-note row**': G, A, C and its **inversion** note, D. This row is taken from the open strings of the cello (C G D A).

This row is used by the composer in different compositional guises. Deane uses the compositional device of the **subtraction** principal to develop his melodic line fully in Section 1.

- The first full statement of the melody (motif) is six notes in length. The violin plays the theme against the inversion of the theme in the cello.
- The second rendition is of five notes, the sixth note being subtracted.
- The third rendition of the theme is of four notes, the last fifth note being subtracted and so on.

The contrary technique of **addition** is also used in the A³ section. The piano accompaniment starts with just one chord and builds to eight chords while the alto flute theme is being reduced, one note at a time.

Augmentation is also used as a compositional device. This is where note values in a motif/theme are made larger than previously heard (Section 3 in the strings).

The open strings can be used in double, triple or quadruple stopping while maintaining the row. Playing on an 'open' string cannot produce vibrato. This effect is eerie and sounds nearly medieval.

Complex rhythmic patterns and rhythmic counterpoint are abundant in this work. Frequently changing time signatures also give the work a vacillating pulse. Deane uses the device of rhythmic displacement and cross rhythms to also help syncopate the pulse.

Harmonic Analysis

The harmonic analysis of the piece follows the general form or structure of the sections:

- overall, it is written in an **atonal** tonality. There is no key centre, but the three-note row (or four-note row including D) is the closest sounding 'tonal' centre in the piece
- the note G is central to the Introduction and Section 1
- the note D is the pedal note (in the cello) in Section 3
- the note E flat is the central note in Section 5
- C major chords (on strings, double stopping) are important in the final section, Section 6 (bi-tonality – other instruments play against the C major chords in dissonance)
- the piece ends on the next most important note, A.

Table 8.12   Analysis of *Seachanges*

Form	Section Name	Features	Bars
A	Introduction	Main melody	1–20
A^1	Section 1	Main melody and inversion	21–45
B	Section 2	Totentanz	46–68
	Link	Development of Totentanz	69–73
A^2	Section 3	Main melody and inversion	74–91
C	Section 4	Dies Irae	92–127
A^3	Section 5	Main melody	128–140
B^1 and C^1	Section 6	Totentanz and Dies Irae	141–174

Glossary of Musical Terms

A niente – to nothing, e.g. to ppp.

A tempo – return to the previous tempo.

Absolute music – music that relies on its structure alone for understanding. Also known as abstract music.

Accelerando, accel. – gradually becoming faster.

Accent – placed above a note to indicate stress or emphasis.

Accidental – a sharp, flat or natural not included in the given key.

Accompaniment – a vocal or instrument part that supports a solo part.

Ad libitum, ad lib – a term which permits the performer to extemporise or vary the music at will.

Adagio – slow; slower than andante, faster than largo.

Agitato – agitated; with excitement.

Al coda – 'to the coda'.

Al fine – to the end.

Alberti bass – an accompaniment pattern of broken, or arpeggiated, chords; named after the eighteenth-century Venetian composer Domenico Alberti.

Aleatory, or aleatoric music – chance music in which the performers are free to perform their own material and/or use their own manner of presentation.

Alla breve – cut time; metre in which there are two beats in each measure and a half note receives one beat.

Allargando, allarg. – slowing of tempo, usually with increasing volume; most frequently occurs toward the end of a piece.

Allegretto – a little slower than allegro.

Allegro – fast.

Alto – a female vocalist with a range between the soprano and tenor parts.

Alto clef – the C clef falling on the third line of the stave. Mostly used by the viola.

Andante – at walking pace. Tempo marking.

Andantino – a little faster than andante.

Animato – animated; lively.

Antiphonal – responsive music usually sung by two groups of singers.

Appoggiatura – a non-chordal tone, usually a semitone or tone above the notated tone, which is performed on the beat and then resolved.

Arpeggio – a term used to describe the pitches of a chord as they are sung or played one after the other, rather than simultaneously.

Atonality – lacking a tonal centre. Music that is written and performed without regard to any specific key.

Augmentation – compositional technique in which a melodic line is repeated in longer note values. The opposite of diminution.

Augmented – the term for a major or perfect interval which has been enlarged by one half-step, e.g. c–g (an augmented fifth) or c–d (an augmented second). Also used for a triad with an augmented fifth, e.g. the augmented tonic triad in C major, C+, c–e–g.

Backbeat – accentuation of beats two and four, usually by a snare drum.

Bar line – the vertical line placed on the stave to divide the music into measures.

Bass – the lowest-pitched member of a family of instruments/lowest voice. Bass also denotes the lowest part in a musical composition.

Bass clef – the other name for the F clef.

Basso continuo, Continuo, Thorough-bass – the baroque practice in which the bass part is played by a viola da gamba (cello) or bassoon while a keyboard instrument performs the bass line and the indicated chords.

Bends – a guitar technique in which a note is altered in pitch by pushing the string up.

Binary form – the term for describing a composition of two sections, AB, each of which may be repeated.

Bitonality – the occurrence of two different tonalities at the same time.

Brass family – Wind instruments made out of metal with either a cup- or funnel-shaped mouthpiece, such as trumpet, cornet, bugle, flugelhorn, trombone, tuba, baritone horn, euphonium and French horn.

Broken chords – notes of a chord played in succession rather than simultaneously. An arpeggio.

C clef – a clef usually centred on the first line (soprano clef), third line (alto clef), fourth line (tenor clef), or third space (vocal tenor clef) of the stave. Wherever it is centred, that line or space becomes middle C.

Cadence – a chordal or melodic progression that occurs at the close of a phrase, section or composition, giving a feeling of a temporary or permanent ending. The four types of cadence are perfect, plagal, imperfect and interrupted.

Cadenza – a solo passage, often virtuosic, usually near the end of a piece, either written by the composer or improvised by the performer.

Call and response – a technique of African folk origin by which a solo singer is answered by a chorus singing a repeated phrase.

Canon – the strictest form of imitation, in which two or more parts have the same melody but start at different points.

Canonic – a term used to describe a polyphonic style of music in which all the parts have the same melody but start at different times.

Cantabile – in singing style.

Cantata – baroque sacred or secular choral composition containing solos, duets, and choruses, with orchestral or continuo accompaniment.

Chamber music – music for a small ensemble.

Chance music – aleatoric music.

Chorale – hymn-like song, characterised by blocked chords.

Chord – a combination of three or more tones sounded simultaneously.

Chromatic scale – a scale composed of twelve semitones.

Classical – usually music composed during the period 1770–1820.

Clef – a symbol placed at the beginning of the stave to indicate the pitch of the notes on the stave. The most commonly used clefs in choral music are the G or treble clef and the F or bass clef.

Coda – closing section of a composition. An added ending.

Coloratura – elaborate, ornamented vocal passage.

Common time – 4/4 metre.

Con – with.

Con brio – with spirit; vigorously.

Con moto – with motion.

Concert pitch – the international tuning pitch – currently A 440 hertz. The pitch for non-transposing (C) instruments.

Concertino – a short concerto. The group of soloists in a concerto grosso.

Concerto – a piece for a soloist and orchestra.

Concordant (consonance) – a satisfied chord or interval; perfect intervals and major and minor thirds and sixths.

Conductor – the person who directs a group of musicians.

Conjunct – pitches on successive degrees of the scale; opposite of disjunct.

Corda, corde – string.

Countermelody – a vocal part that contrasts with the principal melody.

Counterpoint – the technique of combining single melodic lines or parts of equal importance.

Crescendo – gradually become louder.

Cut time – 2/2.metre.

Da capo, D. C. – return to the beginning.

Dal segno, D. S. – repeat from the sign. Frequently followed by al fine.

Decrescendo (decr.) – gradually become softer.

Diatonic – the notes indigenous to a key in a major or minor scale.

Diminished – the term for an interval that has been decreased from the major by a tone and from the perfect by one semitone.

Diminuendo, dim – Gradually become softer. Synonymous with decrescendo.

Diminution – the shortening of note values; the opposite of augmentation.

Disjunct – the term used to describe intervals larger than a second; the opposite of conjunct.

Dissonance (discordant) – sounds of unrest, e.g. intervals of seconds and sevenths; the opposite of consonance.

Distortion – a sound effect that overloads the speaker. Used in rock and heavy metal.

Divisi, div – an indication of divided musical parts.

Dolce – sweetly.

Dolcissimo – very sweetly.

Dominant – the fifth degree of the major or minor scale. Also the term for the triad built on the fifth degree, labelled V in harmonic analysis.

Drone – a continuous accompanying note usually played in the bass.

Duet – a piece for two performers.

Duplet – a group of two notes performed in the time of three of the same kind.

Dynamics – varying degrees of loud and soft.

E – Italian word meaning 'and'.

Echo – often called a 'delay': a sound effect produced by a guitar pedal.

Embellishment – ornamentation.

Enharmonic – a term used to describe notes of the same pitch that have different names, e.g. c# and db, f# and gb.

Espressivo – expressively.

Falsetto – a style of male singing in which, by partial use of the vocal chords, the voice is able to reach the pitch of a female.

Feedback – used mainly by rock musicians to produce a high-pitched sound.

Fermata – hold; pause.

Finale – the last movement of a symphony or sonata, or the last selection of an opera.

Fine – the end.

Fixed doh – the system of solmisation in which c is always doh.

Form – the design or structure of a musical composition.

Forte (f) – loud.

Fortissimo (ff) – very loud.

Fortississimo (fff) – very, very loud.

Forzando (fz), also forzato – synonymous with sforzando (*sf* or *sfz*).

Fugal – a contrapuntal compositional device like a canon

Glissando (gliss.) – sliding, by playing a rapid scale.

Grave – slow, solemn.

Grosso, grosse – great, large.

Harmony – the sounding of two or more simultaneous musical notes in a chord.

Hemiola – switch between metres 3/4 and 6/8.

Homophonic – musical texture characterised by chordal support of a melodic line.

Hook – a memorable part of a song.

Imitation – compositional device involving much repetition by different voices/instruments playing similar material at different times.

Improvisation – music to be invented by the performer on the spot. Used extensively in jazz.

Instrumentation – the art of composing, orchestrating, or arranging for an instrumental ensemble.

Interval – the distance between two pitches. The name of an interval depends both on how the notes are written and the actual distance between the notes as measured in semitones.

Intonation – a manner of producing notes with regard to accurate pitch and tuning.

Inversion – the turning upside-down of a chord or a melodic pattern.

Key signature – the sharps or flats placed at the beginning of the stave to denote the scale upon which the music is based.

Larghetto – slower than largo.

Largo, lento – slow

Leading note – the seventh degree of the major scale.

Ledger lines – short lines placed above and below the stave for pitches beyond the range of the stave.

Legato – smooth, connected.

Leitmotif – a musical theme given to a particular idea or main character of an opera (also, in Berlioz, *idée fixe*)

Libretto – a book of text containing the words of an opera.

Lick – a melodic device based on a musical pattern to form short solos.

Major chord – a triad composed of a root, major third, and perfect fifth.

Marcato – emphasised, heavily accented.

Mediant – the third degree of the major or minor scale. The triad built on this degree is labelled iii in the major scale, and III+ (augmented) in the harmonic minor scale.

Medieval – the period prior to the Renaissance, c. 500–1450; the period of the music of the early Christian church.

Melisma or melismatic – many notes written to one syllable.

Meno mosso – less motion.

Mezzo – half, medium.

Minimalist – style of simple harmonic music with much repetition of phrases.

Mixing stage (in a recording) – reproduces the sound and delays it.

Modal – scales that preceded the development of major and minor scales and tonality; gapped scale, whole tone scale, pentatonic scale.

Moderato – moderate speed.

Modulation – the process of changing from one key to another within a composition.

Molto – very. Used with other terms, e.g. molto allegro.

Mosso – rapid. Meno mosso: less rapid. Più mosso: more rapid.

Motif – a motif is a short musical idea that occurs often in a piece of music. A short melodic idea may also be called a motiv, a motive, a cell, or a figure.

Moto – motion. Con moto, with motion.

Multi-track recording – a technique by which up to 24 tracks can be recorded.

Natural – a musical symbol that cancels a previous sharp or flat.

Non troppo – not too much. Used with other terms, e.g. non troppo allegro: not too fast.

Nonet – a composition written for nine instruments.

Octave – the interval between the first and eighth notes of a scale.

Octet – a piece for eight instruments or voices.

Open fifth – a triad without a third.

Open strings – strings are not stopped, fingered, or fretted.

Opus, Op. – the term, meaning 'work', is used to indicate the chronological order of a composer's works, e.g. Op. 1, Op. 2.

Orchestral music – music written for a large group of instruments. These usually include strings, brass, percussion and woodwinds.

Orchestration – the art of writing, arranging or scoring for the orchestra.

Ornamentation – note or notes added to the original melodic line for embellishment such as trills, mordents, turns or grace notes.

Ostinato – a repeated melodic or rhythmic pattern.

Ottava alta (8va) – play an octave higher.

Ottava bassa (8vb) – play an octave lower.

Overdub – a recording technique in which another part is recorded over a previous part.

Overture – the introductory music for an opera, oratorio or ballet.

Panning – a recording technique in which the pan control allows the sound to be placed.

Passing notes – unaccented notes that move conjunctly between two chords to which they do not belong harmonically.

Pedal note – a long held note (usually tonic or dominant) over which various harmonies occur, producing harmonic tension.

Perfect – a term used to label fourth, fifth, and octave intervals. It corresponds to the major, as given to seconds, thirds, sixths, and sevenths.

Perfect cadence – the chordal progression of dominant to tonic, in a major key V–I, in a minor key V–i.

Perfect pitch – the ability to hear and identify a note without any other musical support.

Pesante – heavily.

Petite – little.

Peu a peu – little by little.

Phrase – a relatively short portion of a melodic line which expresses a musical idea, comparable to a line or sentence in poetry.

Pianissimo (pp) – very soft.

Pianississimo (ppp) – very, very soft; the softest common dynamic marking.

Piano (p) – soft.

Pianoforte – 'soft-loud'. A keyboard instrument, the full name for the piano. It has 88 keys.

Picardy third – the term for the raising of the third, making a major triad, in the final chord of a composition which is in a minor key. The practice originated around 1500 and extended through the baroque period (Tierce de Picardie).

Pick up – a small microphone in an electric guitar or other electric instrument.

Pitch – the highness or lowness of a note.

Più – more. Used with other terms, e.g. più mosso, more motion.

Pizzicato – plucked. On string instruments, plucking the string.

Plagal cadence – sometimes called the 'amen' cadence. The chordal progression of subdominant to tonic, in a major key IV–I, in minor iv–i.

Poco – little. Used with other terms, e.g. poco accel.; also poco a poco, little by little.

Poco più mosso – a little more motion.

Portamento – very smooth transition between two notes (nearly glissando-like).

Postlude – the final piece in a multi-movement work. Organ piece played at the end of a church service.

Powerchords – use of open strings to produce a heavier sound on guitars.

Prelude – an introductory movement or piece.

Premiere – first performance.

Prestissimo – very, very fast. The fastest tempo.

Presto – very fast.

Primo – first.

Programme music – music based on a story, mood or idea.

Prologue – an introductory piece that presents the background for an opera.

Quartet – a piece for four instruments or voices. Four performers.

Quasi – almost. Used with other terms.

Quintet – a piece for five instruments or voices. Five performers.

Rallentando, rall. – gradually slower. Synonymous with ritardando.

Range – the notes, from lowest to highest, that an instrument may be capable of producing.

Refrain – a short section of repeated material which occurs at the end of each stanza.

Register – a specific area of the range of an instrument.

Relative major and minor scales – major and minor scales which have the same key signature.

Repeat – the repetition of a section or a composition as indicated by particular signs.

Rest – a symbol used to denote silence.

Reverberation – a recording technique that creates an echo effect using electronics.

Rhythm – the term that denotes the organisation of sound in time.

Riff – a repeated short phrase like an ostinato in a jazz composition.

Rimshot – drummer hits rim of snare or side drum.

Rinforzando – a reinforced accent.

Ritardando, rit. – gradually becoming slower.

Ritenuto – Immediate reduction in tempo.

Ritmico – rhythmically.

Roll – on percussion instruments, a sticking technique consisting of a rapid succession of notes.

Romanticism – the period c. 1820–1900.

Root position – the arrangement of a chord in which the root is in the lowest voice.

Round – like a canon, a song in which two or more parts have the same melody, starting at different points. The parts may be repeated as desired.

Rubato – the term used to denote flexibility of tempo to assist in achieving expressiveness.

Run – a rapid scale passage.

Rustico – pastoral, rustic, rural.

SATB – soprano, alto, tenor and bass.

Scale – a progression of notes in a stepwise motion in a specific order.

Score – the written depiction of all the parts of a musical ensemble with the parts stacked vertically and rhythmically aligned.

Secco – dry.

Semitone – a half step. The smallest interval on the keyboard.

Semplice – simple.

Sempre – always. Used with other terms, e.g. sempre staccato.

Senza (sans) – without. Used with other terms, e.g. senza crescendo.

Sequence – the repetition of a melodic pattern on a higher or lower pitch level.

Seventh chord – when a seventh (above the root) is added to a triad (root, third, fifth), the result is a seventh chord, e.g. the dominant triad in the key of C major, g–b–d, with the added seventh becomes g–b–d–f and is labelled V7. Much used in rock, soul.

Sforzando (sfz, sf) – sudden strong accent on a note or chord.

Sharp – a symbol (#) that raises the pitch of a note one-half step.

Simile – similar, an indication to continue in the same manner.

Six-four chord – the second inversion of a triad, made by placing the fifth of the chord in the lowest voice.

Slur – a curved line placed above or below two or more notes of different pitch to indicate that they are to be performed in legato style.

Solmisation – the term for the use of syllables for the degrees of the major scale: doh, re, mi, fa, sol, la, ti, doh. The minor scale (natural) is la, ti, doh, re, mi, fa, sol, la.

Solo – a part that is performed alone or as the predominant part.

Sonata – a solo instrumental piece (sometimes with piano accompaniment), often in four movements.

Sostenuto – sustained.

Spiccato – on string instruments, a bowing technique in which the bow is bounced on the string at moderate speed.

Staccato – detached sounds, indicated by a dot over or under a note. The opposite of legato.

Stretto – a contrapuntal compositional device in which imitative parts quickly overlap.

Strophic – a term used to describe a song in which all the stanzas of the text are sung to the same music. The opposite of through-composed.

Subdominant – the fourth degree of the major or minor scale. Also the name of the triad built on the fourth degree of the scale, indicated by IV in a major key and by iv in a minor key.

Subito – suddenly.

Submediant – the sixth degree of a major or minor scale. Also, the name of the triad built on the sixth degree of the scale, indicated by VI in a major key and by vi in a minor key.

Sul – on the (e.g. sul tasto: on the fingerboard).

Supertonic – the second degree of the major or minor scale. Also the name of the triad built on the second degree of the scale, indicated by II in a major scale and ii in a minor scale.

Sur – on, over.

Suspension – the use of a non-chord note to delay the resolution of a chord, frequently as it occurs in a cadence.

Syllabic – one note per syllable.

Symphony – a piece for large orchestra, usually in four movements, in which the first movement is often in sonata form. A large orchestra.

Syncopation – accent on an off beat.

Tanto – much, so much.

Tempo – the rate of speed in a musical work.

Tempo primo – return to the original tempo.

Tenor – instruments in the tenor range. It is between the alto and baritone parts.

Tenuto (ten.) – hold or sustain a note longer than the indicated value.

Ternary form – three-part form in which the middle section is different from the other sections. Indicated by ABA.

Terraced dynamics – the baroque style of using sudden changes in dynamic levels, as opposed to gradual increase and decrease in volume.

Tessitura – the general pitch range of a vocal part.

Texture – the term used to describe the way in which melodic lines are combined, either with or without accompaniment. Types include monophonic, homophonic and polyphonic (contrapuntal).

Theme – a longer section of melody that keeps reappearing in the music. Themes are generally at least one phrase long and often have several phrases. Many longer works of music, such as symphony movements, have more than one melodic theme.

Theme and variations – a statement of a musical subject followed by restatements in different guises.

Through-composed – a term used to describe a song in which the music for each stanza is different. The opposite of strophic.

Tie – a curved line over or below two or more notes of the same pitch. The first pitch is sung or played and held for the duration of the notes affected by the tie.

Timbre – tone colour or quality of an instrument's sound.

Time signature – synonymous with metre.

Tonality – the term used to describe the organisation of the melodic and harmonic elements to give a feeling of a key centre or a tonic pitch.

Tone – sound that has a definite pitch. Any given tone is characterised by length, loudness, timbre and a characteristic pattern of attack and fade.

Tone clusters – the simultaneous sounding of two or more adjacent tones.

Tonic – the first note of a key. Also, the name of the chord built on the first degree of the scale, indicated by I in a major key or i in a minor key.

Tranquillo – tranquilly; quietly; calm.

Transposition – the process of changing the key of a composition.

Treble – the highest instrument part. A boy soprano.

Treble clef – the G clef falling on the second line of the stave.

Triad – a chord of three tones arranged in thirds, e.g. the C major triad c-e-g, root-third-fifth.

Trill, tr – a musical ornament performed by the rapid alternation of a given note with a major or minor second above.

Triplet – a group of three notes performed in the time of two of the same kind.

Tritone – a chord comprising three whole tones resulting in an augmented fourth or diminished fifth.

Troppo – too much. Used with other terms, e.g. allegro non troppo, not too fast.

Turnaround – a small harmonic phrase that links two sections or repeats of a piece.

Tutti – all. A direction for the entire ensemble to sing or play simultaneously.

Twelve-tone technique (serial music) – a system of composition that uses the twelve tones of the chromatic scale in an arbitrary arrangement called a tone row or series. The row may be used in its original form, its inversion, in retrograde, and in the inversion of the retrograde. The system was devised by Arnold Schoenberg in the early twentieth century.

Un peu – a little. Used with other words, e.g. un peu piano.

Un poco – a little.

Una corda – soft pedal (left pedal on piano).

Unison – singing or playing the same notes by all singers or players, either at exactly the same pitch or in a different octave.

Upbeat (anacrusis) – one or more notes occurring before the first bar line.

V.S. or Volti subito – turn [the page] quickly.

Variation – the development of a theme by the use of melodic, rhythmic, and harmonic changes.

Vibrato – repeated fluctuation of pitch.

Virtuoso – a brilliant, skillful performer.

Vivace – lively, brisk, quick, and bright.

Vivo – lively, bright.

Wah wah – a guitar pedal that varies the pitch of the note.

Wind instruments family – instruments in which sound is produced by the vibration of air, including brass and woodwind instruments.

Woodwind family – instruments, originally made of wood, in which sound is produced by the vibration of air, including recorders, flutes, clarinets, saxophones, oboes, cor anglais and bassoons.

Exam Papers

Coimisiún na Scrúduithe Stáit
State Examinations Commission

LEAVING CERTIFICATE EXAMINATION 2005

MUSIC – HIGHER LEVEL

LISTENING – CORE (100 marks)

THURSDAY 23 JUNE – MORNING, 9.30 to 11.00

Q. 1   An excerpt from *Piano Quartet No. 1* by Gerald Barry.
- The full excerpt will be played ONCE only. Section A, B and C, taken from this excerpt, will then be played THREE times.
- Answer the questions on pages 103–104.

Section A, Bars 1–26, and its repeat.

Section B, Bars 53–107. On the recording, the melody below (bars 53–70) will be played three times.
The repeats are not notated.

Section C, Bars 108–154. There is no printed music for this section.

Section A, Bars 1–26, and its repeat.

(i)   Name the tune on which this excerpt is based. _ _ _ _ _ _ _ _ _ _ _ _ _ _ _

(ii)   Describe the use of canon in this excerpt.

_ _

_ _

(iii) Fill in the missing notes, played by the violin, on the score in bars 4 and 5.

Section B, Bars 53–107.

(i)   The tune is heard three times in this excerpt. Describe two ways in which the *first* playing of the tune differs from the *third*. Refer to both playings in your answer.

_ _

_ _

_ _

_ _

(ii)   Fill in the missing time signatures in bars 60, 61 and 62.

Section C, Bars 108–154. There is no printed music for this section. On the recording the melody is played three times.

     (i)   Identify and describe an instrumental technique heard in this excerpt.

          _____

          _____

     (ii)   The *second* time the melody is heard, it is played

        ❑ an octave lower   ❑ at the same pitch   ❑ an octave higher

     (iii) Describe Barry's use of Irish melodies in his *Piano Quartet No. 1*.

          _____

          _____

          _____

          _____

(25)

Q.2   An excerpt from Cantata 78 *Jesu, der du meine Seele* by Bach will be played THREE times.

    ■   There will be a suitable pause after each playing.

    ■   The outline score is printed below.

■ Answer the following questions.

(i) Name the type of voice which sings the melody line in this excerpt

_____

Name TWO instruments which double the melody line in this excerpt.

1. _____   2. _____

(ii) The key of this movement is

❏ B♭ major   ❏ D minor   ❏ G minor   ❏ G major

(iii) Insert the missing rhythm and melody notes on the score in bars 11 and 12.

(iv) Which of the following can be heard in the *continuo* part in bars 13–14?

❏ stepwise movement   ❏ off-beat crotchets   ❏ broken chords

(v) Identify the cadences at **X** and **Y.**

X _____   Y _____

(10)

Q. 3 An excerpt from *Bohemian Rhapsody* by Queen will be played THREE times.
■ There will be a suitable pause after each playing.
■ The lyrics are printed below.
1 Mama, just killed a man, Put a gun against his head
2 Pulled my trigger, now he's dead.
3 Mama, life had just begun, But now I've gone and thrown it all away.
4 Mama, ooh, Didn't mean to make you cry.
5 If I'm not back again this time tomorrow, carry on.
6 Carry on as if nothing really matters.

■ Answer the following questions.

(i) Name the TWO instruments which accompany the singer in lines 1 and 2.

1. _____   2. _____

(ii) Circle the word in the text where the cymbals are heard for the first time.

(iii) Identify TWO features of the accompaniment in this excerpt.

_____

_____

(iv) Describe TWO ways in which the music of the *next* verse differs from the verse heard in this excerpt. Refer to *both* verses in your answer.

1 _____

_____

_____

2 _____

_____

_____

(v)   Identify TWO recording techniques used in *Bohemian Rhapsody.*

1. _____   2. _____

(10)

Q. 4 An excerpt from the *Romeo and Juliet Fantasy Overtune* by Tchaikovsky will be played THREE times.

■ There will be a suitable pause after each playing.

■ The outline score of bars 1–4 of the excerpt is printed below.

■ Answer the following questions.

(i)   From which section of the work is this excerpt taken? _____

(ii)   The theme heard in this excerpt is known as _____

(iii) Describe ONE rhythmic feature of this theme.

_____

_____

(iv)   A canon is heard towards the end of the excerpt. Identify TWO instruments which play in canon.

1. _____   2. _____

Which of the following is played by the violins during the canon?

❑ broken chords   ❑ semiquaver scale passages

❑ syncopated rhythms.

(v)   The style of this work is Romantic. Identify and describe two features of this style which are present in this overture.

_____

_____

_____

_____

_____

(10)

Q.5   **Irish Music.** Answer A and B. Note that B contains a choice of questions.

A.   You will hear THREE excerpts, each played THREE times.

Excerpt 1

(i)   Name the two instruments playing the melody.

1. _____   2. _____

Name one instrument playing the accompaniment. _____

(ii)   Identify this type of dance tune and its time signature.

Dance: _____   Time signature: _____

(iii)   Write two bars of rhythm associated with this type of dance.

_____

Excerpt 2

(i)   Identify the style of singing in this excerpt. _____

(ii)   Name three features of this style of singing heard in this excerpt.

1 _____

2 _____

3 _____

(iii)   The range of the music in this excerpt is

❏ a sixth   ❏ an octave   ❏ more than an octave

Excerpt 3

(i)   Using letters, write down the form of the verse _ _ _ _ _ _ _ _ _ _ _ _ _ _

(ii)   Identify four instruments in this excerpt.

    1. _ _ _ _ _ _ _ _ _ _ _ _ _ _   2. _ _ _ _ _ _ _ _ _ _ _ _ _ _ _

    3. _ _ _ _ _ _ _ _ _ _ _ _ _ _   4. _ _ _ _ _ _ _ _ _ _ _ _ _ _

(iii)   Describe TWO differences between the arrangements of verse 1 and verse 2.
        You must refer to *both* verses in your answer.

    _

    _

    _

    _

    _

B.   Answer ONE of the following.

(i)   Discuss regional performing styles in the context of Irish traditional music. In
        your answer, refer to a performer from each of the regions which you
        mention and to specific musical examples.

OR

(ii)   Give an account of the Irish jig, reel and hornpipe. In each case, refer to the
        time signature, rhythm and structure. Include a musical example for each
        dance.

OR

(iii)   Write an account of a group you have studied in the context of Irish
        traditional music. In your answer, refer to the style of music performed by the
        group and to specific musical examples.

OR

(iv)   Discuss some of the developments that have taken place in Irish traditional
        music in the 20th century. In your answer, refer to specific musical examples.

(25)

Q. 6 **Aural Skills.** This question is based on the *Hallelujah* chorus from Handel's oratorio
        Messiah.

    ▪ The full excerpt will be played ONCE only. Sections A, B and C, taken from
        this excerpt, will then be played THREE times.

    ▪ Answer the questions on each section.

Section A

- The first 8 bars sung by SATB choir are printed below. They are preceded by an orchestral introduction.

(i) How many bars of music are played in the introduction before the choir begins to sing? _____

(ii) The rhythm of the bass part at X is

(iii) Circle one bar on the score above where syncopation occurs.

Section B

- The first 11 bars of the second section are printed below.

(i)   The voices in bar 12 sing in

❑ unison   ❑ thirds   ❑ fifths

(ii)   Complete the eight missing melody notes in bars 17–19 on the score.

(iii)   Which brass instrument sometimes doubles the melody in this section?

Section C

■ The opening lyrics of the text are printed below.

■ There is no printed music for this section.

Line 1:   The Kingdom of the world is become

Line 2:   The Kingdom of our Lord and of His Christ, and of His Christ

Line 3:   And He shall reign for ever and ever…

(i)   Identify two ways in which the music of line 2 differs from the music of line 1.

        _____

        _____

(ii)   In which order do the voices (sopranos, altos, tenors, basses) enter starting at
        line three – 'And He shall reign for ever and ever'?

        1. _____   2. _____

        3. _____   4. _____

(iii)   Describe how Handel conveys a triumphant mood in this section.

        _____

        _____

        _____

        _____

        _____

        _____

Coimisiún na Scrúduithe Stáit
State Examinations Commission

LEAVING CERTIFICATE EXAMINATION 2005

MUSIC – HIGHER LEVEL

LISTENING – ELECTIVE (100 marks)

THURSDAY 23 JUNE – MORNING, 11.15 TO 12.00

Answer ALL questions.

1.   State the title of your chosen Listening Elective topic.

_____

_____

2.   List three valid sources which you used in studying this topic. (Note: *Full* details are required for your sources. If one of your sources is the internet, give the full website address used in your search.)

(i)   _____

(ii)   _____

(iii)   _____

3.   Name five pieces of music and the composer or performer, which you studied as part of this elective, and which are on your tape.

Piece	Composer or Performer
1.	
2.	
3.	
4.	
5.	

4. (a) List three important *musical* features of your chosen topic.

(i)   _____

(ii)   _____

(iii)   _____

(b) Write an account of your chosen topic describing the three musical features which you have identified above. Show how these, and other musical features, are present in some or all of the music you have studied. In your answer, refer to the music on your tape **and** include your personal response to your chosen topic.

_____

_____

_____

_____

_____

Coimisiún na Scrúduithe Stáit
State Examinations Commission

LEAVING CERTIFICATE EXAMINATION 2005

MUSIC – HIGHER LEVEL

COMPOSING (100 MARKS)

THURSDAY 23 JUNE – AFTERNOON, 2.00 TO 3.00

Answer TWO questions – ONE from Section A (Melody Composition) and ONE from Section B (Harmony)

SECTION A – MELODY COMPOSITION (40 marks)

Answer ONE QUESTION ONLY *in this section:* Q1 *or* Q2 *or* Q3.

Q.1 CONTINUATION OF A GIVEN OPENING
- Continue the opening below to make a 16-bar melody.
- Add appropriate performing directions (phrasing and dynamics) to the melody.

- Choose a suitable instrument for your melody from the following list:

❏ flute   ❏ violin   ❏ oboe   ❏ accordion

❏ horn   ❏ trumpet

(40)

Q.2 SETTING MUSIC TO A GIVEN TEXT

Here is an excerpt from *The Road Goes Ever On (The Lord of the Rings)* by J.R.R. Tolkien.

The road goes ever on and on
Down from the door where it began
Now far ahead the road has gone,
And I must follow if I can.

- The opening line has been set to music below.
- Set the remaining words to make a melody of 16 bars. (Your may exceed this number of bars, and include a modulation, if you wish.)
- Add appropriate performing directions (phrasing and dynamics).

The _ Road __ goes   ev - er   on __   and   on

(40)

Q.3   COMPOSING TO A GIVEN DANCE RHYTHM OR METRE OR FORM

The opening phrase of a gigue is given below.

- Continue the given opening to make a 16-bar melody.
- Use the form AA¹BB¹.
- Include a modulation to the dominant at a suitable point.
- Add appropriate performing directions (phrasing and dynamics).
- Choose a suitable instrument for your melody from the following list:

❑ violin   ❑ oboe   ❑ flute   ❑ glockenspiel   ❑ piccolo

(40)

SECTION B – HARMONY (60 marks)

Answer ONE QUESTION ONLY *in this section:* Q4 *or* Q5 *or* Q6

Q.4   COMPOSING MELODY AND BASS NOTES FROM A SET OF CHORDS
PREPARATORY WORK
- Plot the chords available in the key of B$^\flat$ major, either in the chord band grid *or* on the stave below.

Notes of chord	F D B♭	G E♭ C_m	A F D	B♭ G E♭	C A F	D B♭ G_m	E♭ C A
Chord symbol	B♭	C_m	D_m	E♭	F	G_m	A_dim
Roman numeral	I	ii	iii	IV	V	vi	vii

I   ii   [iii]   IV   V   vi   [vii]

- Study the following piece of music
- Using the chords indicated, compose melody and bass notes to complete the piece in the given style.

imperfect

I   V_b   I   V₇   vi   IV   V

B♭   F/A   B♭   F7   Gm   E♭   F

interrupted

I_b   I   vi   IV   ii   V   vi

B♭/D   B♭   Gm   E♭   Cm   F   Gm

(60)

Q.5 COMPOSING BASS NOTES AND CHORD INDICATIONS TO A GIVEN TUNE

PREPARATORY WORK

- Plot the chords available in the key of A♭ major, either in the chord band grid *or* on the stave below.

Notes of chord	E♭ C A♭		G E♭ C				D♭ B♭ G
Chord symbol	A♭		C_m				G_{dim}
Roman numeral	I	ii	iii	IV	V	vi	vii

I   ii   [iii]   IV   V   vi   [vii]

Study the following song and insert suitable bass notes and chord indications in the style of the given opening.

■ Do *not* repeat the same chord *in the same position* in adjacent boxes.

■ You may use chord symbols or Roman numerals, but not both.

■ If you choose Roman numerals, use *lower case* for *minor* chords.

(60)

Q.6 ADDING A COUNTERMELODY OR DESCANT AND CHORDAL SUPPORT TO A GIVEN TUNE.

PREPARATORY WORK

- Plot the chords available in the key of D major, either in the chord band grid *or* on the stave below.

Notes of chord	A F♯ D	C♯ A F♯			G E C♯
Chord symbol	D	F♯m			C♯dim
Roman numeral	I	ii	iii	IV	V	vi	vii

Study the following piece of music.

- Insert suitable chord indications in the boxes provided and continue the descant part in the given style to complete the piece.
- You may use chord symbols or Roman numerals, but not both.
- If you choose Roman numerals, use *lower case* for *minor* chords.
- Do *not* repeat the same chord *in the same position* in adjacent boxes.

(60)

LC Music 2005 Marking Scheme Core Listening Paper – Higher level

Q	Sec	Part	Answer	Mark	Sub-total	Total
1	**A**	(i)	Sí Bheag, Sí Mhór (2)	2		
		(ii)	4-part canon; @ 8ve; crotchet distance; vln., vla, vc., pno (L.H.); 5-part canon; @ 8ve; crotchet distance; pno (L.H.), pno (R.H.), vc, vla, vln. **Any 3 components** (3)	3		**9**
		(iii)	♩♩♩♩ ♩♩ .5 mark per correct pitch. **Up to 2 marks for contour**	.5 x 8		

B

(i) 1. Melody on vln accompanied by vla (2-note / 5-note   2+2
   rhythmic figure); *forte*; roughly; senza vibrato; polyphonic;

   3. melody at 3 different 8ves on vln, vla, vc and pno
   clusters; *fff*; very little vibrato; explosively; higher pitch;   **7**
   vc & pno also playing; homophonic;
   Up to 2 marks for each of any two differences;

(ii)   🎵 (1 x 3)   1+1+1

1

C

(i) senza vibrato; cello harmonics; roughly; detached; savagely   1+2   **25**
   1 mark for identification. Up to 2 marks for description

(ii) An octave lower (2)   2

(iii) Section 1 (A): Sí Bheag, Inversion of Sí Mhór; canon   1+3
   Last section (H): Lord Mayo's Delight; canon   **9**
   All sections have rhythms and melodies derived from A;
   use of jig rhythm.
   Any valid reference to Irish characteristics.
   .5 mark for each named tune. Up to 3 marks for good description.

2

(i) Soprano (.5)   .5   1.5
   flt / ob / organ / vln / horn (.5 + .5)   .5+.5

(ii) G minor   .5   .5

(iii) 🎵 **Up to 1 mark per bar**   2+2   4   **10**
   for each of melody and rhythm.

(iv) Stepwise movement (1)   1   1

(v) **X** = imperfect (I–V) (1.5)   **Y** = Perfect (V–I) (1.5)   1.5+1.5   3
   Either title or chords accepted
   Incorrect chords cancel out correct title or v.v.

Q	Sec	Part	Answer	Mark	Sub-total	Total
		(i)	Pno (.5) Bass / bass gtr (.5)	.5+.5	1	
		(ii)	'away'–end of line 3 (1)	1	1	
3		(iii)	Arp. / broken chords on pno; b.gtr & L.H. pno play 1 note per bar (root); b.gtr. gliss. after 'trigger now he's dead'; 2–note fig. crotchet on pno; pno. mirrors vocal part at 'just begun'; I–vi–ii–V; chromatic descending bass at 'thrown it all away' and 'mean to make you cry'; drums play standard rock pattern from 'Mama . . ooh'; cymbal crashes at 'didn't mean to make you cry'; **1 mark for each of 2 identifications.**	1+1	2	**10**
		(iv)	**Verse 1:** no drums at start; no word painting; no lead gtr.; no panning; solo voice; **Verse 2:** drums in from start; bell tree / gtr effect, word painting at 'shivers down my spine'; lead gtr.; gradual panning; backing vocals; **Up to 2 marks for each of two descriptions.**	2+2	4	
		(v)	stereo; panning; layering; multi-tracking; double tracking; overdubbing; reverb; flangeing (1 + 1)	2	2	
		(i)	Exposition (1)	1	1	
		(ii)	1st subject / strife / Montagues & Capulets (.5)	.5	.5	
4		(iii)	syncopated / dotted rhythm; tutti rhythm; dactyl; **1.5 marks for correct statement or description**	1.5	1.5	**10**
		(iv)	**1.** vc. / cb (1) **2.** picc. / flt. / ob / cl (1) Semiquaver scale passages (1)	1+1+1	3	
		(v)	Large orchestra; rich orchestral texture; rich harmonies; variety of tone colour; programme music; **1 mark for each of two identifications. 1 mark for each description.**	2+2	4	
	A 1	(i)	flt (.5) vln (.5) banjo	.5+.5 .5		
		(ii)	jig (.5) 6/8 (.5)	.5+.5		
5		(iii)	.5 for each of 2 bars of jig rhythm	.5+.5		
	A 2	(i)	sean nós; traditional Irish; Donegal style; (.5)	.5		
		(ii)	ornamentation; free rhythm; little / no dynamics; nasal tone; unaccompanied solo performance; wide range; regional characteristics; **1 mark for each of 3 features.**	1+1+1		
		(iii)	more than an 8ve (1)	1		

Q	Sec	Part	Answer	Mark	Sub-total	Total
5	**A 3**	(i)	ABBA	1	**15**	
		(ii)	gtr; pipes; flt; bass; pno/keyboard; vln; harp; tin whistle; **.5 mark for each of 4 correct instruments**	.5 x 4		
		(iii)	**Verse 1:** unison singing; acc. by harp block chords; thin texture; **Verse 2:** 3-pt harmony; descant; gtr, pipes, flt, tin whistle, bass, pno, vln added; full texture; flowing acc.; moving quavers **Up to 2 marks for each of 2 descriptions.**	2+2		**25**
5	**B**		Up to 10 marks for quality of answers and knowledge of topic chosen. See descriptors below. *Deduct up to 3 marks for quality and relevance of appropriate references.*		**10**	
		A	Excellent awareness and detailed knowledge of musical features of topic.	10		
		B	Very good knowledge of musical features of chosen topic.	8–9		
		C	Good knowledge of topic, but lacking in detail.	6–7		
		D	Some general points on topic, but lacking sufficient detail.	4–5		
		E	Generally inadequate response to chosen topic.	2–3		
		F	Little response to chosen topic in evidence.	1		
		NG	No response to chosen topic in evidence.	0		
6	**A**	(i)	3 (2)	2	**5**	
		(ii)	Rhythm 3 (2)	2		
		(iii)	Bar 4 (1) 2	1		
	B	(i)	Unison (1)	1	**6**	
		(ii)	.5 for each of 8 correct pitches	.5 x 8		
		(iii)	Trumpet (1)	1		

Q	Sec	Part	Answer	Mark	Sub-total	Total
		(i)	**Line 2:** louder; pitched higher; no rest in middle of phrase; timpani and trumpet added; brief transition to A; **Up to 2 marks for each of 2 differences**	2 + 2		
		(ii)	1. bass (.5) 2. tenor (.5) 3. alto (.5) 4. soprano (.5)	.5 x 4		
6	C	(iii)	*f* and *ffi* dynamics; long held notes; repetition; use of rests; rich instrumentation; use of tpt and timp.; augmented 'halleluia' at end; sustained notes; repetition of 'for ever' and 'halleluia'; polyphony; sop / alto v. tenor / bass; rising melody; word painting; unison rhythms at end; *Any other valid description.* **Up to 3 marks for one valid description.**	3	9	**20**

LC Music 2005 Marking Scheme Listening – Higher level – elective

Element	Question	Descriptors	Mark	Sub-total	Total
Tape		10 relevant extracts / No marks if tape obviously dubbed / For extracts significantly over 30 seconds, deduct .5 mark each	10	**10**	
	1	Name of topic	–		
	2	Relevant and appropriate sources	–		
	3	Five relevant pieces	–		
Paper	4	A Excellent awareness and detailed knowledge of musical features of topic. Well-researched, with appropriate personal response.	77–90		
		B Very good knowledge of musical features of chosen topic. Well researched, but personal response less well developed.	63–76		
		C Chosen topic lacks sufficient focus. Good knowledge of musical features of chosen topic, but lacking in detail. Some evidence of personal response. Adequate research in evidence.	50–62		

Element	Question		Descriptors	Mark	Sub-total	Total
Paper	**4**	D	Some general points on topic, but lacking any detail. Very little evidence of research or personal response. Choice of topic too broad to allow for appropriate detailed and personal response. Little reference to musical features of topic.	36–49	**90**	**100**
		E	Generally inadequate response to chosen topic. No evidence of research or personal response.	23–35		
		F	Little response to chosen topic in evidence.	9–22		
		NG	No response to chosen topic in evidence.	0–8		

Deduct up to 5 marks for quality of sources at Question 2

Deduct up to 5 marks (1 mark per piece) for omission of 5 relevant pieces at Question 3

Deduct up to 5 marks for non-reference or inadequate reference to taped extracts and named pieces at Question 4.

LC Music 2005 Marking Scheme Composing – Higher level – core

Question		Descriptors	Mark	Total
1	A	Melody has style and imagination. Very aware of shape and structure. Excellent development of opening ideas. Very good points of climax.	34–40	**40**
	B	Good sense of shape and structure. Musical, with good point(s) of climax. Opening ideas well developed.	28–33	
	C	A good sense of melodic and rhythmic interest. Points of rest outlined. Good development of opening ideas with a sense of structure and good technical knowledge.	22–27	
	D	A fair sense of shape and some awareness of balance between phrases. Reasonable sense of structure and technical knowledge.	16–21	
	E	Some melodic and rhythmic interest. Little sense of structure or technical knowledge. Poor shape.	10–15	
	F	No shape, sense of structure or technical knowledge.	0–9	

Deductions, if omitted or deficient: *Phrasing (structural / articulation / both), dynamics, instrument (up to 2 each). Accept one correct instrument only (clef & range)*

Question		Descriptors	Mark	Total
2	A	Showing excellent style and imagination with a convincing 'marriage' of words and music.	34–40	
	B	Melodically and rhythmically convincing with a good sense of words, music and climax.	28–33	
	C	Good sense of melody writing with careful word setting. Good sense of climax.	22–27	**40**
	D	Awareness of shape and balance between phrases. Some sense of climax. Reasonable sense of technical knowledge and word setting.	16–21	
	E	Some melodic interest and sense of key. An attempt at word setting. Little sense of technical knowledge. Poor shape.	10–15	
	F	No shape. Almost non-existent word setting.	0–9	

Deductions, if omitted or deficient: *Phrasing, dynamics* **(up to 2 each).**

Question		Descriptors	Mark	Total
3	A	Melody has style and imagination. Very aware of shape and structure. Excellent development of opening ideas. Very good points of climax. Rhythmic integrity and style of dance maintained with flair. Excellent adherence to given structure.	34–40	
	B	Good sense of shape and structure. Musical, with good point(s) of climax. Opening ideas well developed. Rhythmic integrity and style of dance well maintained. Very good adherence to given structure.	28–33	
	C	A good sense of melodic and rhythmic interest. Points of rest outlined and good development of opening ideas. Rhythmic integrity of dance fairly well maintained. Good adherence to given structure.	22–27	**40**
	D	A fair sense of shape and some awareness of balance between phrases. Good attempt at maintaining dance rhythm. Reasonable sense of technical knowledge. Fair adherence to given structure.	16–21	
	E	Some melodic and rhythmic interest. Little sense of structure or technical knowledge. Poor shape. Very little awareness of dance rhythm. Little adherence to given structure.	10–15	
	F	No shape, sense of structure or technical knowledge. No sense of appropriate dance rhythm. No adherence to given structure.	0–9	

Deductions, if omitted or deficient: *Modulation at a suitable point (4), Phrasing (structural / articulation / both), dynamics, instrument (up to 2 each) Accept one correct instrument only (clef & range)*

Question	Element		Descriptors	Mark	Sub-Total	Total
	Bass		.5 mark per correct bass note under each chord symbol if treble melody note is also correct.	10.5	**20**	
			Quality of bass line, including continuing in style of given opening.	9.5		
4	**Melody**	A	Melody has style and imagination with an excellent awareness of underlying harmonic structure and development of opening ideas. Very good sense of climax.	34–40	**40**	**60**
		B	Good sense of shape and structure. Musical, with a good awareness of harmonic structure and good point(s) of climax. Opening ideas well developed.	28–33		
		C	A good sense of melodic and rhythmic interest and awareness of harmonic structure. Points of rest outlined and good development of opening ideas.	22–27		
		D	A fair sense of shape and balance between phrases. Notes generally fit chords.	16–21		
		E	Some melodic and rhythmic interest. Little sense of structure. Some notes fit chords.	10–15		
		F	No shape. Very few notes fit chords.	0–9		
5	**Chords**		1 mark for each chord that is part of a good progression.	24	**36**	**60**
			Quality of progressions overall No marks for chord if suffix omitted / minor chords not indicated correctly or any accidental omitted. Dominant may be followed by Dominant 7th.	12		
	Bass		.5 mark per correct bass note under each correct chord symbol in boxes 2–23. 1 mark for correct bass note under box 24. Chord symbol and bass note must match.	12	**24**	
			Quality of bass line, including continuing in style of given opening, and also including up to 2 marks for note placement throughout.	12		
6	**Chords**		1 mark for each chord that fits melodic line and is part of a good musical progression. Up to 4 marks for awareness of cadences. Bass notes need not be indicated.	16+4	**20**	

Question	Element		Descriptors	Mark	Sub-Total	Total
		A	Excellent continuation of descant style within harmonic framework.	34–40		
		B	Very good melodic line, which fits well over harmonic structure. Two-part style of given opening well maintained.	28–33		
		C	Good melodic line and shape. Melody fits harmonic structure. Good attempt at maintaining two-part style of opening.	22–27		
6	**Descant**	D	Notes generally fit chords. Some attempt at maintaining style. Fair sense of shape and balance between phrases.	16–21	**40**	**60**
		E	Some notes fit chords. Little attempt at maintaining style. Little sense of structure. Little sense of technical knowledge.	10–15		
		F	Very few notes fit chords. No effort at maintaining style. Very poor technical knowledge.	0–9		

LC Music 2005   Marking Scheme   Composing – Higher level – elective

	Descriptors	Mark	Total
A	Very creative and original, with good grasp of the principles of composition, orchestration or arranging. Appropriately notated and including a detailed description of the compositional process.	85–100	
B	A good degree of creativity and originality, displaying good control of compositional skills, appropriately notated. Good description of compositional process.	70–84	
C	An acceptable degree of originality, with adequate control of musical features, appropriately notated. Fair description of compositional process.	55–69	**100**
D	Basic understanding of composition with little evidence of originality. Adequate notation and description of compositional process.	40–54	
E	Material presented shows little evidence of elementary compositional skills. Inadequate notation. Description lacks any detail of compositional process.	25–39	
F	Little or no value. Composition not notated. No description of compositional process included.	0–25	

Coimisiún na Scrúduithe Stáit
State Examinations Commission

LEAVING CERTIFICATE EXAMINATION 2004

MUSIC – HIGHER LEVEL

LISTENING – CORE (100 marks)

THURSDAY 24 JUNE – MORNING, 9.30 to 11.00

Q. 1 An excerpt from Mozart's *Piano Concerton in A major K488*.
- You will hear it without a break and then each section (A, B and C) will be played again THREE times.
- The music is given as a reduced, single line score below for sections A and C only. There is no printed music for section B.
- Answer the questions on pages 130–31.

Section A, bars 1–12

Section B, bars 12–20 There is NO printed music for this section.

Section C, bars 20–42

Section A, bars 1–12

(i)   Identify the movement from which this excerpt is taken _ _ _ _ _ _ _ _ _ _

(ii)   Identify the key in which this excerpt is written   _ _ _ _ _ _ _ _ _ _ _ _ _

(iii) What is the tonality of the broken chord played in bar 10? _ _ _ _ _ _ _ _

       This chord spans

       ☐ an octave   ☐ an octave and a fifth   ☐ two octaves

Section B, bars 12–20

(i)   Describe TWO features of the music in this section.

       1. _

           _

           _

           _

       2. _

           _

           _

           _

Section C, 20–42

(i) This section begins with the piano.
     In which bar are more instruments added? _ _ _ _ _ _ _ _ _ _ _ _ _ _ _ _

     These instruments are

     ❏ strings only   ❏ strings and brass   ❏ strings and woodwind

(ii) The melody introduced at **X** (bars 35–36) is repeated at **Y** (bars 39–40).
      Identify ONE difference between the music heard at **X** and at **Y.**

      _

      _

(iii) Briefly describe what happens in the coda of this movement.

      _

      _

(25)

Q.2 An excerpt from *Sergeant Pepper's Lonely Hearts Club Band* by the Beatles will be
played THREE times.

■ There will be a suitable pause after each playing.

■ The words of the excerpt are printed below.

Line 1   We're Sergeant Pepper's Lonely Hearts Club Band

Line 2   We hope you will enjoy the show

Line 3   Sergeant Pepper's Lonely Hearts Club Band

Line 4   Sit back and let the evening go.

Line 5   Sergeant Pepper's Lonely, Sergeant Pepper's Lonely

Line 6   Sergeant Pepper's Lonely Hearts Club Band

Line 7   It's wonderful to be here. It's certainly a thrill.

Line 8   You're such a lovely audience.

Line 9   We'd like to take you home with us, we'd love to take you home.

■ Answer the question below.

(i) Which brass instruments play in the 5-bar opening of this excerpt?

     _

     These brass instruments play

     ❏ in unison   ❏ in contrary motion   ❏ independent melodic lines

(ii)   The music of line 1 is printed below. Fill in the missing notes in bars one
        and two.

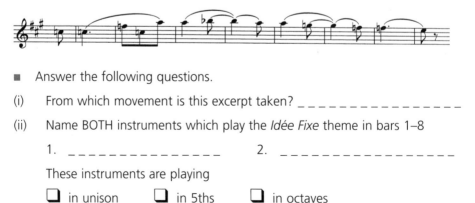

We're Ser - geant Pep - pers Lone - ly   Hearts Club   Band.   We hope you will en - joy the   show.—

(iii)   The dominant bass rhythm is lines 1–4 is

(iv)   Describe ONE way in which the accompaniment changes in lines 7–9.

        _____

        _____

(v)   The style of this song is a fusion of pop/rock and classical. Describe how both
        of these styles are used in this song.

        _____

        _____

        _____

        _____

                                                                                            (10)

Q. 3   An excerpt from *Symphonie Fantastique* by Berlioz will be played THREE times.
        ■ There will be a suitable pause after each playing.
        ■ The outline score of bars 1–8 of the excerpt is printed below.

        ■ Answer the following questions.
(i)   From which movement is this excerpt taken? _ _ _ _ _ _ _ _ _ _ _ _ _ _ _

(ii)   Name BOTH instruments which play the *Idée Fixe* theme in bars 1–8

        1. _ _ _ _ _ _ _ _ _ _ _ _ _   2. _ _ _ _ _ _ _ _ _ _ _ _ _

        These instruments are playing

        ❑ in unison   ❑ in 5ths   ❑ in octaves

(iii) The theme is played in

❏ A major ❏ F major ❏ C major

(iv) Describe any TWO features of the accompaniment in this excerpt

1. _____

_____

_____

_____

2. _____

_____

_____

_____

(v) Identify ONE other place where the *Idée Fixe* theme is played in *Symphonie Fantastique* and describe ONE way in which it differs from the excerpt player here.

_____

_____

_____

(10)

Q. 4 An excerpt from *Seachanges (with Danse Macabre)* by Raymond Deane will be played THREE times.
- There will be a suitable pause after each playing.
- Answer the following questions.

(i) From which section of the work is this excerpt taken? _____

(ii) Which of these percussion instruments is heard first?

❏ tambourine ❏ maracas ❏ bass drum

(iii) Describe the manner in which the piano plays towards the end of the excerpt.

_____

_____

_____

(iv) Which of the following is the correct notation for *'play the harmonic'*?

Explain the term harmonic and name any instrument which plays harmonics in this excerpt.

Explanation _____

_____

_____

Instrument _____

(v)   State ONE way in which this excerpt contrasts with the next section of this work.

_____

_____

_____

_____

(10)

Q. 5   Irish Music. Answer A and B. Note that B contains a choice of questions.
A.   You will hear THREE excerpts, each played THREE times.
Excerpt 1 An arrangement of *Down By The Sally Gardens* by WB Yeats.

(i)   This recording is a fusion of traditional music with

❑ pop   ❑ folk   ❑ classical

Give a reason for your answer.

_____

_____

(ii)   Using letters, write down the form of the *verse*. _____

Excerpt 2

(i)   Name the instrument playing the melody.   _____

(ii)   Which ONE of the following can be heard in the recording?

❑ changing dynamics   ❑ free rhythm   ❑ minor melody

(iii)   This melody is an example of a

❑ polka   ❑ march   ❑ lament

(iv)   Give a reason for your answer

_____

_____

Excerpt 3

(i)   Name THREE instruments which play the melody in this excerpt.

1. _ _ _ _ _ _ _ _ _ _ _ _ _ _ _   2.   _ _ _ _ _ _ _ _ _ _ _ _ _ _ _

3. _ _ _ _ _ _ _ _ _ _ _ _ _ _

(ii)   This recording is a fusion of two different styles. Identify and describe BOTH
        styles, as heard in this excerpt.

_ _

_ _

_ _

_ _

B. Answer ONE of the following.

(i)   What contribution has traditional Irish music made to the folk music of North
        America? Refer to specific music examples in your answer.

OR

(ii)   Give an account of the contribution made to traditional Irish music by Sean
        O'Riada. Support your answer with references to compositions, styles and
        performers, as appropriate.

OR

(iii)   In the context of Irish traditional music, describe a work, or movement of a
        work, by a 20th century composer that uses traditional Irish elements in
        his/her music. Refer to appropriate musical examples in your answer.

OR

(vi)   Write an account of *sean nós* singing in the Irish language. Refer to
        performers in your answer.

(25)

Q.6   Aural Skills. This question is based on a piece of film music, *The Dambusters,* by
         the British composer, Eric Coates.
■   The full excerpt will be played ONCE only. Sections A, B and C, taken from
      the excerpt, will then be played THREE times, unless otherwise stated.
■   Answer the question on each section.

Section A
■   The first 16 bars of the first theme are printed below.

(i)   What word best describes the way in which the melody is predominantly played?

☐ *doloroso*   ☐ *staccato*   ☐ *tenuto*

(ii) The melody is imitated by lower strings. Indicate clearly on the score with an **X** above the exact point at which the imitation begins.

(iii) What effect does the rhythm at **Y** create?

Section B

■ All of the second theme is printed below.

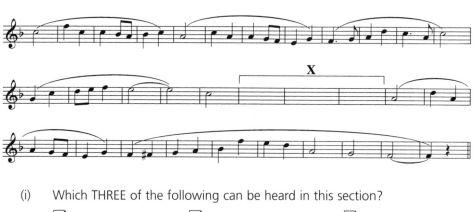

(i)   Which THREE of the following can be heard in this section?

☐ countermelody   ☐ woodwind figures   ☐ tremolo

☐ legato playing   ☐ pizzicato bass line   ☐ pedal notes

(ii) Complete the melody by filling in the missing notes at **X** on the score.

■ This theme is now repeated, played differently. It will be played TWICE. Answer part (iii).

(iii) Identify TWO ways in which this music differs from the first time it was heard.

1 _____

2 _____

Section C

■ The music for the final section is printed below.

(i)   Which type of drum plays a roll at **X**? _

(ii)   Identify the cadence heard at **Y** _

(ii)   The notes repeatedly played by the timpani at **Z** are

(20)

Coimisiún na Scrúduithe Stáit
State Examinations Commission

LEAVING CERTIFICATE EXAMINATION 2004

MUSIC – HIGHER LEVEL

LISTENING – ELECTIVE (100 marks)

THURSDAY 24 JUNE – MORNING, 11.15 TO 12.00

Answer ALL questions.

1. State the title of your chosen Listening Elective topic.

    _____

    _____

2. List three valid sources which you used in studying this topic (Note: If one of your sources is the internet, give the full website address used in your research.)

    (i)   _____

    (ii)   _____

    (iii)   _____

3. Name five pieces of music and the composer or performer, as appropriate, which you studied as part of this elective, and which are on your tape.

Piece	Composer or Performer
1.	
2.	
3.	
4.	
5.	

4.   (a)   Identify three important musical features of your chosen topic.

(i)   _____

(ii)   _____

(iii)   _____

(b)   Write an account of your chosen topic describing the musical features you have identified above. Show how these and other musical features are present in some or all of the music you have studied. In your answer, refer to the music on your tape and include your personal response to your chosen topic.

_____

_____

_____

_____

_____

Coimisiún na Scrúduithe Stáit
State Examinations Commission

LEAVING CERTIFICATE EXAMINATION 2004

MUSIC – HIGHER LEVEL

COMPOSING (100 MARKS)

THURSDAY 24 JUNE – AFTERNOON, 2.00 TO 3.00

Answer TWO questions – ONE from Section A (Melody Composition) and ONE from Section B (Harmony)

SECTION A – MELODY COMPOSITION (40 marks)

Answer ONE QUESTION ONLY *in this section:* Q1 *or* Q2 *or* Q3.

Q.1   CONTINUATION OF A GIVEN OPENING
■   Continue the opening below to make a 16-bar melody.
■   Include a modulation to the dominant at a suitable point.
■   Add appropriate performing directions (phrasing and dynamics) to the melody.

- Choose a suitable instrument for your melody from the following list:

  ❑ violin   ❑ horn   ❑ flute   ❑ bassoon   ❑ trumpet

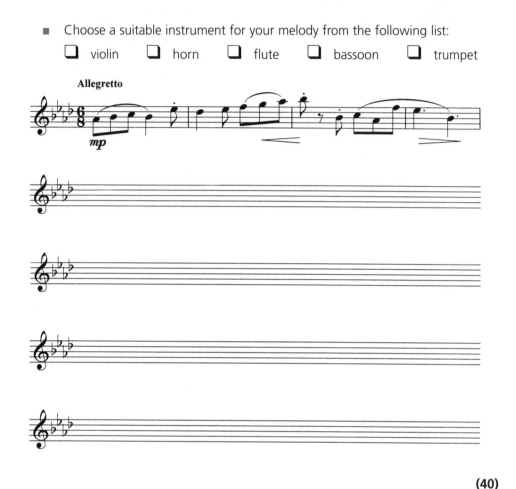

(40)

Q.2   SETTING MUSIC TO A GIVEN TEXT

Here is an excerpt from *Lullaby* by Thomas Dekker.

Golden slumbers kiss your eyes.
Smiles awake you when you rise,
Sleep pretty wantons do not cry,
And I will sing a lullaby.

- The opening line has been set to music below.
- Set the remaining words to make a melody of 16 bars. (Your may exceed this number of bars, and include a modulation, if you wish.)
- Add appropriate performing directions (phrasing and dynamics).

Golden slumbers kiss your eyes.

(40)

Q.3 COMPOSING TO A GIVEN DANCE RHYTHM OR METRE OR FORM

The opening phrase of a minuet is given below.

- Continue the given opening to make a 16-bar melody.
- Use the form AA^{1}BA^2.
- Add appropriate performing directions (phrasing and dynamics).
- Choose a suitable instrument for your melody from the following list:

    ❏ violin   ❏ treble recorder   ❏ flute   ❏ trumpet   ❏ horn

(40)

SECTION B – HARMONY (60 marks)

Answer ONE QUESTION ONLY *in this section* Q4 *or* Q5 *or* Q6

Q.4   COMPOSING MELODY AND BASS NOTES FROM A SET OF CHORDS
PREPARATORY WORK
   ■   Plot the chords available in the key of A minor, either in the chord band grid
       or on the stave below.

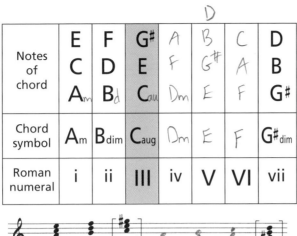

- Study the following piece of music.
- Using the chords indicated, compose melody and bass notes to complete the piece in the given style.

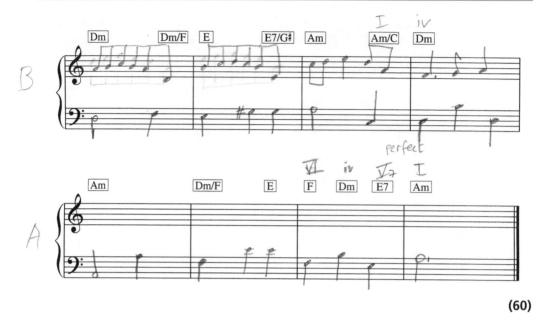

(60)

Q.5   COMPOSING BASS NOTES AND CHORD INDICATION TO A GIVEN TUNE
PREPARATORY WORK
- Plot the chords available in the key of C minor, either in the chord band grid *or* on the stave below.

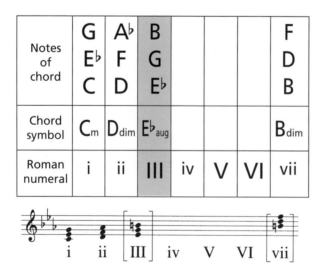

Notes of chord	G E♭ C	A♭ F D	B G E♭				F D B
Chord symbol	C$_m$	D$_{dim}$	E♭$_{aug}$				B$_{dim}$
Roman numeral	i	ii	III	iv	V	VI	vii

Study the following song and insert suitable bass notes and chord indications in the style of the given opening.
- Do *not* repeat the same chord *in the same position* in adjacent boxes.
- You may use chord symbols or Roman numerals, but not both.
- If you choose Roman numerals, use *lower case* for *minor* chords.

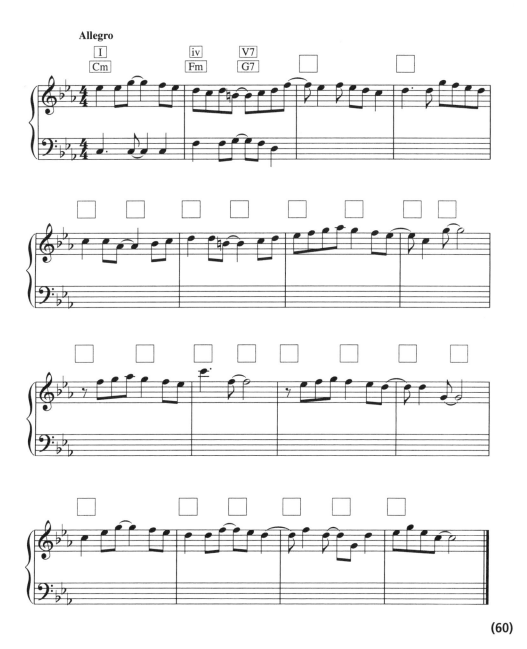

(60)

Q.6 ADDING A COUNTERMELODY OR DESCANT AND CHORDAL SUPPORT TO A GIVEN TUNE.

PREPARATORY WORK

- Plot the chords available in the key of F major, either in the chord band grid *or* on the stave below.

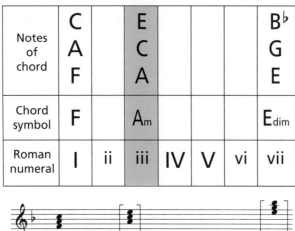

Study the following piece of music.

■ Insert suitable chord indications in the boxes provided and continue the descant part in the given style to complete the piece.

■ You may use chord symbols or Roman numerals, but not both.

■ If you choose Roman numerals, use *lower case* for *minor* chords.

■ Do *not* repeat the same chord *in the same position* in adjacent boxes.

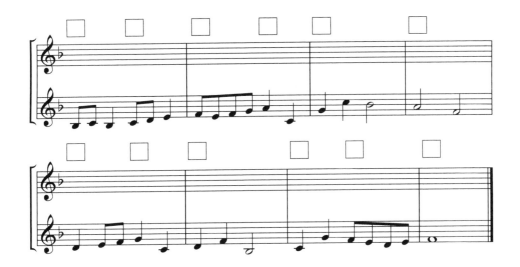

(60)

LC Music 2004 Marking Scheme Core Listening Paper – Higher level

Q	Sec	Part	Answer	Mark	Sub-total	Total
		(i)	2nd movement/Adagio (2)	2		
	A	(ii)	F# minor (2)	2	**8**	
		(iii)	Major / G major (2); An octave and a fifth (2) 2	2+2		
	B		Imitation / canon in melody between flt. / vln. 1 and fag; Dynamics: very expressive, crescendo; Combination of polyphonic texture in melody and homophonic in accompaniment; Alberti accompaniment/figure in 2nd vln; Dominant pedal in vla; Simple bass line: quavers on 1st and 2nd beats; Texture richer as more instruments added; Tutti as opposed to solo in previous section *Any other valid description* Up to 4 marks for each description of any two features.	4+4	**8**	
1						**25**
		(i)	Bar 25 (2) Strings only (1)	2+1		
	C	(ii)	X: Melody in flt; harmony in 3rds in clt; simple bass line; no other strings; triplet semiquaver arpreggio/broken chord / alberti fig. in 2nd clt; no brass, pno, fag. Y: Melody in 1st clt, pno R.H. and flt (8ve higher without specifying flt (1); higher (.5) *Any other valid point;* Any *one* point. Identification only. (2) Reference to both extracts must be made for full marks.	2	**9**	
		(iii)	Pizzicato string arpeggios / broken chords; i – VI – iv – ic – Va; fragments of 1st subject (Ib) on fl, cl. and fag.; music fades to *pp;* comments on pno; Any other valid point; Up to 4 marks for good description.	4		
		(i)	French horns (.5) + independent melodic lines (5)	.5+.5	1	
		(ii)	1 for each of 5 correct notes (pitch and rhythm)	5	5	
		(iii)	rhythm no. 2 (1)	1	1	
2		(iv)	smoother; less driven; arpeggio in bass; sustained chords on horns; drums ease back; *Any other valid point.* (1)	1	1	**10**
		(v)	Pop/rock: instrumentation (lead, rhythm, bass guitars, drums); driving bass; rhythm; chord sequences; vocal style; sound effects; *Any other valid point* (1) Classical: instrumentation (horns); vocal harmony; contrapuntal texture; *Any other valid point.* (1)	1+1	2	

Q	Sec	Part	Answer	Mark	Sub-total	Total
		(i)	2nd movement/Un Bal (1)	1	1	
		(ii)	Flute (.5); oboe (.5); in unison (1)	.5 +.5+1	2	
		(iii)	F major (1)	1	1	
3		(iv)	Tremolando in upper strings; descending and ascending arpeggios/broken chords in vc and cb. Vln 1 and 2 answer each other; vamping in lower strings; fragments of subject (I or II) heard in canon/imitation in vln1 and vla; dominant pedal in the bass. *Any other valid point.* Up to 2 marks for each description of any two features.	2+2	4	**10**
		(v)	mvt 2: bars 302–319 (coda); melody on cl over dominant pedal in horn and harp arpeggios at end of phrase. mvt.4: melody in clt unaccompanied. 4/4 time. mvt.1: medoly unacc. In flt and vln 1. mvt.3: melody in flt and cl in imitation; 6/8 time; accompanied. mvt.5: melody in Eb cl; 6/8 time; ww only; grace notes. 1 mark for identifying correct place; 1 mark for description of difference. Both themes must be referred to.	1+1	2	
		(i)	Introduction	1	1	
		(ii)	Maracas	1	1	
		(iii)	*ff* descending arpeggios/broken chords; reference to effect created;	1	1	
4		(iv)	Example 1; (1) A secondary note (from the harmonic series) which sounds in sympathy with a fundamental note when played; touching a string lightly at specific points so that only the secondary note sounds. *Any valid description* (1) Violin; vc. Either one (1)	1+1+1	3	**10**
		(v)	Fragmented introduction of 3-note cell v main theme; Free rhythm v steady rhythm and more structured feel; Changes of time sig. v no changes of time sig. Very few harmonics v almost all harmonics; 3-note cell (GAC) inverted to GFD; much percussion v very little percussion *Any other valid point* Up to 4 marks for description. Both sections must be referred to for full marks.	4	4	

Q	Sec	Part	Answer	Mark	Sub-total	Total
5	**A 1**	(i)	Folk (1): broken chord guitar acc.; simple style; sung lightly with very gentle ornamentation; range of song not too wide; (1)	1+1		
		(ii)	AABA (1)	1		
	A 2	(i)	Uilleann pipes/pipes (1)	1		
		(ii)	Free rhythm (1)	1		
		(iii)	Lament (1): slow tempo; free rhythm; "personal" feel; words known (Táimse im' chodladh). Any one (2)	1+2	**15**	
	A 3	(i)	Piano; oboe; violins; flt / piccolo / whistle; 1 mark each for any three. (3)	1+1+1		**25**
		(ii)	Trad. (1): jig rhythm; ornamentation; flattened 7th; syncopated style of playing ; use of bodhrán/spoons/bones; any other valid point (1) Classical (1): instrumentation (orchestral); classical harmonies; changes of key; any other valid point (1) Jazz (.5): pno style of playing; syncopated rhythm; any other valid point (1) 1 mark for each of two identifications; 1 mark for each description.	2+2		

Q	Sec	Part	Answer	Mark	Sub-total
5	**B**		Up to 10 marks for quality of answers and knowledge of topic chosen. See descriptors below. *Deduct up to 3 marks for quality and relevance of appropriate references.*		
		A	Excellent awareness and detailed knowledge of musical features of topic.	10	
		B	Very good knowledge of musical features of chosen topic	8–9	**10**
		C	Good knowledge of topic, but lacking in detail.	6–7	
		D	Some general points on topic, but lacking sufficient detail.	4–5	
		E	Generally inadequate response to chosen topic.	2–3	
		F	Little response to chosen topic in evidence.	1	
		NG	No response to chosen topic in evidence.	0	

Q	Sec	Part	Answer	Mark	Sub-total
6	**A**	(i)	Staccato (1)	1	**5**
		(ii)	Bar 2 last quaver (2) Due to a potential difficulty with the quality of the recording in this section, accept anywhere in bar 2 or 3	2	
		(iii)	Precise reference to effect on listener (2) or Syncopation; explanation of syncopation (2)	2	

Q	Sec	Part	Answer	Mark	Sub-total	Total
		(i)	Countermelody + legato playing + pizzicato bass line (1 + 1 + 1)	3		
		(ii)	.5 mark for each of 7 correct pitches. Rhythm must be correct.	3.5		
6	**B**	(iii)	Melody on strings (vlns) v. melody on brass (tpts / tbns); Countermelody on horns v. different countermelody on vlns. at higher pitch; No fanfare at beginning v. fanfare at beginning; Smooth v. more forceful and accented; 2nd extract louder than 1st; Up to 2 marks for each of two correct answers. Both sections must be referred to for full marks. (2+2)	2+2	**10.5**	**20**
	C	(i)	Snare drum (1.5)	1.5		
		(ii)	Interrupted cadence (2); V – vi (1);	2	**4.5**	
		(iii)	Example 3 (1)	1		

LC Music 2005 Marking Scheme – Higher level Composing – core

Question		Descriptors	Mark	Total
	A	Melody has style, structure, shape and imagination. Excellent exploration and development of opening ideas. Very good points of climax.	34–40	
	B	Very aware of shape and structure. Very musical and good point(s) of climax. Opening ideas well developed.	28–33	
1	**C**	A good sense of melodic and rhythmic interest. Points of rest outlined and good development of opening ideas. Good sense of structure and technical knowledge.	22–27	**40**
	D	A fair sense of shape and some awareness of balance between phrases. Reasonable sense of structure and technical knowledge.	16–21	
	E	Some melodic and rhythmic interest. Little sense of structure of technical knowledge.	10–15	
	F	Very poor shape and very erratic. No sense of structure or technical knowledge.	0–9	

Deductions, if omitted or deficient: Modulation at a suitable point (4), phrasing (structural/articulation/both), dynamics, instrument (up to 2 each). Accept one correct instrument only (clef & range)

Question		Descriptors	Mark	Total
2	**A**	Showing excellent style and imagination. Very original with a convincing 'marriage' of words and music.	34–40	**40**
	B	Melodically and rhythmically very convincing, with good sense of words and music. A convincing climax.	28–33	
	C	Good sense of melody writing with careful word setting. Some originality. Good sense of climax.	22–27	
	D	Awareness of sharpe and balance between phrases. Some sense of climax. Reasonable sense of technical knowledge and work setting	16–21	
	E	Some melodic interest and sense of key. An attempt at word setting. Little sense of technical knowledge.	10–15	
	F	Very poor melodic sharpe and very erratic. Almost non-existent word setting.	0–9	

Deductions, if omitted or deficient: Phrasing, dynamics (up to 2 each).
If existing tune is used, allow up to 5 marks only for fitting words/syllables to notes, tempo and dynamics.

Question		Descriptors	Mark	Total
3	**A**	Melody has style, shape and imagination. Excellent exploration and development of opening ideas. Very good points of climax. Rhythmic integrity and style of dance maintained with flair. Excellent adherence to the given structure.	34–40	**40**
	B	Very aware of shape and structure. Very musical and good point(s) of climax. Opening ideas well developed. Rhythmic integrity and style of dance well maintained. Good adherence to the given structure.	28–33	
	C	A good sense of melodic and rhythmic interest. Points of rest outlined and good development of opening ideas. Rhythmic integrity of dance fairly well maintained. Good adherence to the given structure.	22–27	
	D	A fair sense of shape and some awareness of balance between phrases. Good attempt at maintaining dance rhythm. Reasonable sense of technical knowledge. Fair adherence to the given structure.	16–21	
	E	Some melodic and rhythmic interest. Little sense of structure or technical knowledge. Very little awareness of dance rhythm. Little adherence to the given structure.	10–15	
	F	Very poor shape and very erratic. No sense of appropriate dance rhythm. No adherence to the given structure.	0–9	

Deductions, if omitted or deficient: Phrasing (structural / articulation / both), dynamics, instrument (up to 2 each) Accept one correct instrument only (clef & range)

Question	Element		Descriptors	Mark	Sub-Total	Total
	Bass		.5 mark per correct bass note under each chord symbol if treble melody note is also correct in boxes 1–8 and 10–19.	9+1	**20**	
			Quality of bass line, including continuing in the style of given opening.	10		
4	**Melody**	A	Melody has style, shape and imagination with an excellent awareness of underlying harmonic structure and development of opening ideas. Very good sense of climax.	34–40	**40**	**60**
		B	Very aware of shape and structure. Very musical, with a very good awareness of harmonic structure and good point(s) of climax. Opening ideas well developed.	28–33		
		C	A good sense of shape and balance between phrases. Notes generally fit chords.	22–27		
		D	Very poor shape and very erratic. No sense of structure or technical knowledge.	16–21		
		E	Some melodic and rhythmic interest. Little sense of structure. Some notes fit chords.	10–15		
		F	Very poor shape and very erratic. Very few notes fit chords.	0–9		

Question	Element	Descriptors	Mark	Sub-Total	Total
5	**Chords**	1 mark for each chord that is part of a good progression.	24	**36**	**60**
		• *Due to a printing error in the first chord of the given part, the following instruction has been applied: Where a candidate uses roman numerals exclusively, and where (a) all chords other than i have been notated correctly and (b) all chords of i have been notated with upper case, accept upper case as correct.*			
		Quality of progressions overall NB No marks for chord if suffix omitted / minor chords not indicated correctly, or any accidental omitted. Dominant and dominant 7th may be used in adjacent boxes.	12		
	Bass	.5 mark per correct bass note under each correct chord symbol. Chord symbol and bass note must match.	12	**24**	
		Quality of bass line, including continuing in style of given opening, and also including up to 2 marks for note placement throughout.	12		
6	**Chords**	1 mark for each chord that fits the melodic line and is part of a good musical progression. Up to 2 marks for awareness of cadences. Bass notes need not be indicated.	18+2	**20**	**60**
	Descant	**A** Excellent continuation of descant style within harmonic framework.	34–40	**40**	
		B Very good melodic line that fits well over harmonic structure. Two-part style of given opening well maintained.	28–33		
		C Good melodic line and shape. Melody fits harmonic structure. Good attempt at maintaining two-part style of opening.	22–27		
		D Notes generally fit chords. Some attempt at maintaining style. Fair sense of shape and balance between phrases.	16–21		
		E Some notes fit chords. Little attempt at maintaining style. Little sense of structure. Little sense of technical knowledge.	10–15		
		F Very few notes fit chords. No effort at maintaining style. Very poor technical knowledge.	0–9